# JOURNEY ROUND TURKEY

# JOURNEY ROUND TURKEY

## Guy Arnold

CASSELL

First published in the UK 1989
by Cassell Publishers Ltd
Artillery House, Artillery Row, London SW1P 1RT

Copyright © Guy Arnold 1989

Distributed in the United States by
Sterling Publishing Co. Inc.
387 Park Avenue South, New York, NY 10016-8810

Distributed in Australia by
Capricorn Link (Australia) Pty Ltd
PO Box 665, Lane Cove, NSW 2066

**British Library Cataloguing in Publication Data**
Arnold, Guy, 1932–
  Journey round Turkey.
  1. Turkey. Description & travel
  I. Title
  915.61′0438

ISBN 0–304–31611–3

All photographs are by Guy Arnold

Phototypeset by Input Typesetting Ltd, London

Printed in Great Britain by Richard Clay Ltd, Bungay, Suffolk

# Contents

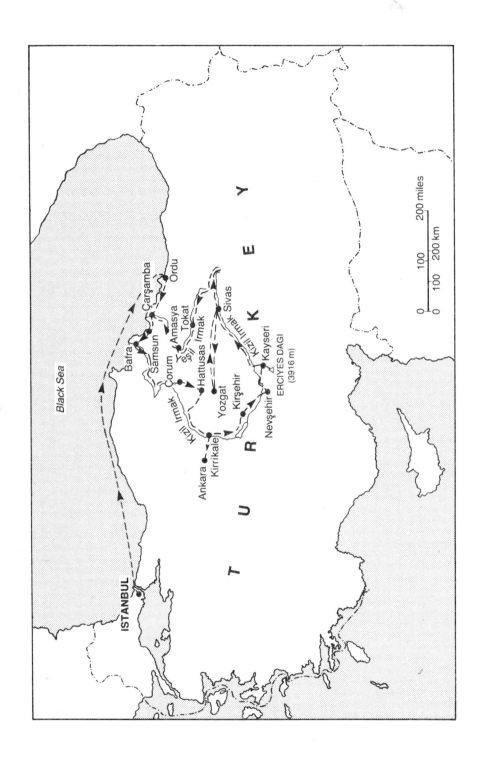

# Introduction

A travel book is a very personal thing. I have always been intrigued by Turkey, which possesses three of the principal ingredients that give both excitement and interest to any travel narrative: rugged and spectacular scenery; a fiercely independent yet friendly people; and an ancient history. At one level I simply wanted to travel in Turkey, yet some kind of discipline is necessary and so I chose to take two rivers which create a circle in the centre of Turkey and use them as my line of march, the guidelines and parameters of my journey.

The Kizil Irmak, the Halys of the ancient world, is the longest river in Turkey. It forms a great curve across the centre of the country and in ancient times acted as the boundary between the Lydian and the expanding Persian Empires. Croesus misinterpreted the famous oracle which told him that if he crossed the Halys a great empire would fall: he crossed the river to oppose the Persians and his empire of Lydia fell to Cyrus the Great.

In his history Herodotus described the Halys as follows:

The boundary between the Median and Lydian empires was the river Halys, which flows from a mountain region in Armenia through Cilician territory, and then, passing between the Matieni and Phrygians, turns northward and forms the boundary between the Cappadocians to the east and the Paphlagonians to the west. The Halys is thus the boundary of nearly the whole of southern Asia Minor from the Mediterranean in the neighbourhood of Cyprus and the Black Sea.

The much shorter Yeşil Irmak is the Iris of antiquity. Part of its course runs along the old caravan route from the Black Sea (Amisus) to Baghdad. Its source, like that of the larger river, lies in the Anatolian mountains to the east of Sivas, but its course to the Black Sea is far more direct.

G.A.

# 1

# Curiosity

I always find it difficult when people ask me why I want to go somewhere. There are plenty of obvious answers about travel: a country is interesting because of its history; the people are attractive; and the scenery is magnificent – each of these reasons is good up to a point but they do not really answer the question. Why that particular part of Turkey? I once came across an exciting description of the Yeşil Irmak passing through its great gorge of Amasya and have wanted to visit that ancient city ever since. On another occasion I got stranded in the south of Turkey without any money and had to hitch across it to Istanbul. That was an exciting journey, the bleak mountain land exercised an abiding attraction for me, the people I then met showed all the curiosity, humour and hospitality for which the Turks are justly famous and ever since I have wanted to return.

Turkey is an old land striving to be modern. Few places on earth have so much history. It accumulated in layers as one ancient civilisation imposed itself upon another. Central Anatolia was the heartland of the great Hittite Empire in the second millenium BC. That was swept into oblivion by the migrating Sea Peoples about 1200 BC. Phrygia, Lydia, Cappadocia, Pontus, each, in their time, thrived in Anatolia; the Persians, the Greeks, Alexander the Great, and the Romans left their marks upon the land. The Byzantine Empire gave way to the Seljuk Turks who in turn were replaced by the Ottoman Turks. And modern Turkey is the creation of Atatürk. I can think of no other country in the world where a leader 50 years dead is as revered as is Atatürk still. Every town has a statue or bust of him prominently displayed and those where there is a convenient hill or rock available – just about every town in the land – have a silhouette of his head picked out in lights to be lit up at night. His impact must have been extraordinary.

It is important to dispel stereotypes. At school I was taught history by a marvellous crusty old Fabian: but though he could not quite repress his satisfaction that the Turks had blocked the overland route to the riches of the East for expanding capitalist Europe he also spoke automatically of the *cruel* Turks, a false stereotype they have long been accorded by European Christians.

My plan was to begin on the Black Sea coast at the mouth of the Kizil Irmak, the longest river whose course is wholly within Turkey, and follow its general line to the head-waters in the mountains beyond Zara and then return to the Black Sea coast, but this time by following the Yeşil Irmak downstream. The Kizil Irmak (red river) was the Halys of the ancient world; the Yeşil Irmak (green river) the former Iris. The area which they enclose is about the size of England: near its centre on bleak hills are the awesome remains of Hattusas, the capital of the Hittite Empire. Amasya was the capital of the Pontic kings, at Zile Julius Caesar won a great victory and then gave posterity his boast: *veni, vidi, vici.* There are reminders of an ancient history throughout the area, whose people are farmers with a lifestyle which, except for the coming of the tractor, can have altered little in many generations.

Apart from taking the two rivers as rough guides for my route I did little planning. At the Royal Geographical Society I obtained photostats of large-scale maps of the area, long out of date, and these proved of little value when I got to Turkey. Instead I relied upon modern maps designed principally for tourists in motor cars. I took an old Austrian army backpack and a second shoulder-bag in which to carry my camera. I wished to be able to walk whenever I chose and pared down my luggage to a minimum but I was in no sense rigid: I did not have to walk and often travelled by bus, though sometimes when I wanted to walk I was unable to do so because friendly Turks insisted upon giving me a lift. I had no precise timetable: sometimes I moved quite swiftly from one town or point to the next, at others I lingered. Scenically, Turkey is a stunning country and as soon as I left the coast at Bafra I rose sharply into the hills. Hills, indeed, were to dominate much of the journey. I travelled during July, August and September and for almost all that time temperatures were well into the eighties (Fahrenheit). Some of the town where I stopped have been settled since ancient times and few places were without traces of a long and exciting past.

I wanted to be vague: I had a general plan, following my two rivers, but that was all. Otherwise I was interested in history and the people and determined to let things happen as they would. In the event this vagueness worked well although it is the antithesis of my normal working temperament, when I become enraged at the less-than-exact behaviour of others.

Before I left London someone asked whether I would not be lonely making such a trip by myself. The answer to this was a double 'no'. I am in any case a loner and often spend time and ingenuity escaping the attentions of others. In Turkey all I had to do was alter the tempo at which I operated. My normal routine in London consists of writing to meet deadlines, lecturing and attending various meetings so that I am part of a constant round of activities, many of which recur with all too frequent regularity. Travelling in Turkey on my own I had time for contemplation and as my journey progressed I did not even feel the need to read, an activity to which I normally devote a good deal of my time. But secondly, the many Turks I met made it impossible for me to be lonely: at the sight of a stranger Turks are ready with a greeting to be followed by hospitality and conversation which all too often takes the form of inquiry.

This brings me to the subject of curiosity. I once gave a dinner party at which I placed my sister-in-law, Mavis, beside Harish, an Indian friend of mine. At the end of the evening when all the other guests had gone Mavis expressed her astonishment that in all the time I had known Harish – about ten years – I had never told him that my father had been born in Calcutta. She could not understand how I could have an Indian friend and not communicate this information to him. I was equally amazed that she felt it mattered. I considered the fact of my father's birthplace totally irrelevant to what Harish and I had in common. I think other people consider me to be secretive. People always want to know your business, even though the knowing will not make any difference except that possession of knowledge about you makes them feel better. I resist such inquisitiveness and this brings me to Turkey. Before leaving London I discussed my proposed trip with a Turkish acquaintance and asked her whether I should have any difficulty in getting strangers to talk with me. 'No,' she said, 'Turks are very curious.' That, as I was to discover, was a monumental understatement. I was forced to adjust my own normal approach to other people's curiosity to the constant inquiries that I was subject to wherever I went. Sometimes people were amazed and intrigued at the appearance of a foreigner in a small town or village where tourists rarely came and were determined to find out all about me, which they did while plying me with tea. Sometimes it was a more basic peasant inquisitiveness: what was I doing in *their* village? And sometimes the persistence of the questions I met with verged upon rudeness. Yet, no matter what the form of the inquiry, Turkish curiosity ensured that I had many opportunities to talk with many different Turks: peasants, truck drivers, farmers, businessmen, shopkeepers or the waiters in cafés, and towards the end when I had got used to the form that our discussions were likely to take I would try to twist the conversation so that I was asking questions about their lives rather than the other way round. They did not often let me get away with that.

Modern tourism is about seeing places and things. Travel is about people. Turks would often ask me why I wanted to visit a particular place since there were no sights or old historic buildings there for me to see. Sometimes they would express astonishment that I had stopped in some small *ordinary* little village: what was the point? The point for me was the people, small farmers, peasants, shopkeepers going about their daily business and allowing me, just a little, to see what their lives were like. Once when I was in the courtyard of an old historic mosque a man buttonholed me so as to deliver a lecture – one that I think he had prepared for all foreigners – and made the point that western tourists were all *objective* (by which he meant they only wished to see things) while Turks, influenced by Islam, were all *subjective* (by which he meant they were only interested in people). I got quite angry with him, first because I did not consider myself to be a tourist, and second because I had spent many hours with people in out-of-the-way places where the chances of being *objective* in his sense did not exist.

# 2

# Istanbul

Istanbul rather than Rome is my eternal city. The great walls of Theodosius which protected the capital of the eastern Roman Empire for a thousand years still stand. And lying squat, heavy and magnificent on its skyline is the world's most evocative church, the Hagia Sophia. Gibbon's description of the siege of Constantinople is one of the finest passages in literature. Before the final assault Mohammed II 'the Great Destroyer', told his army: 'The city and the buildings are mine; but I resign to your valour the captives and the spoil, the treasures of gold and beauty.' On the fall of the city Mohammed, who had prevented one of his soldiers from defacing it, had the huge church of St Sophia transformed into a mosque which it remained until in the present century Atatürk turned it into a museum.

Istanbul is possessed of an essential seediness which is the essence of an exciting city. In *Greenmantle* John Buchan makes it a shadowy, dirty place of spies and the bizarre 'Companions of the Rosy Hours'. Graham Greene, the great charm of whose novels is their abiding seediness, presents the city at the end of *Stamboul Train* rather through his forlorn, offbeat characters than by means of descriptive writing. The city naturally suggests itself as a backdrop to murder: it has featured in the novels of Agatha Christie and Anthony Burgess and whether in the James Bond film, *From Russia with Love*, or Peter Ustinov's *Topkapi* provides wonderful scenic material for any kind of drama.

It has always been important. The setting is strategic; it is also spectacular. The Emperor Diocletian first saw the need to divide the Roman Empire into its Western and Eastern halves, for by his reign the whole had become unmanageable as a single unit and the Eastern empire had become the richer more populous part, requiring an emperor of its own. It was his successor, Constantine the Great, who consolidated this decision by the creation of his great city on the site of the ancient Greek foundation of Byzantium. As Constantinople the city maintained the Roman tradition for a thousand years as the capital of the Byzantine Empire. So strong was that tradition that the Seljuk Turks who conquered Asia Minor but failed to capture the city called their new domains the Empire of Rum after Rome. And when Constantinople fell to the Ottoman Turks in 1453 the event was long seen in Christian Europe as a major catastrophe. In the nineteenth century during the decline of the Ottoman Empire, Britain's ambassador, Stratford de Redcliffe, became known to the Turks as The Great Elchi (Ambassador) and for many years he conducted Britain's eastern policy from the grand neo-classical embassy which is now a mere consulate. And today, though Atatürk moved the seat of government to Ankara, Istanbul remains the most exciting city in Turkey. It is still the country's capital in everything but name.

When I arrived in Istanbul in mid-July it was so hot that I began to wonder about the wisdom of walking in remoter parts of the country with a pack on my back. I could barely cover more than a few hundred metres in the busy, dusty streets without stopping at one of the little roadside kiosks for a drink of lemonade but this served less to slake my thirst than to make me perspire.

I had had my own adventure in Istanbul many years before when, penniless, I had lived on someone else's balcony off one of the rooms of the new Hilton Hotel. That had been part of a young man's adventure and the romance of Istanbul has never worn off. So I spent three days quartering the city by foot. I think one guidebook says that 44 mosques grace the Istanbul skyline, and it is certainly a city of mosques, possessing some of the grandest, most magnificent examples in the world. But it also has Roman and Byzantine treasures such as the aqueduct of Valens, the underground cisterns or the church of Eirene. In the Topkapi Palace I managed to enter by a wrong door to find myself alone in the splendours of the Harem where one is only supposed to go as a member of a guided group.

The great church of St Sophia looks somehow squat from outside and its true proportions only become apparent from within. I can think of no other interior which gives such a sense of time: built by the Emperor Justinian to represent the Divine Wisdom, its massive stones and the huge pillars which support the world's finest dome seem set to remain through eternity.

But the real delight of Istanbul resides in its bustling millions. The streets are always crowded, the traffic chaotic, the noise incessant, and I spent hours wandering through the labyrinth of the covered bazaar or in the winding streets below the huge complex of the Süleymaniye mosque. I had some shopping to do. I found a series of army surplus stores and purchased a water bottle which could be attached to my belt and a floppy hat. I never normally wear anything on my head but I decided that I should need some protection against the sun of central Anatolia. I needed a few other oddments such as soap and obtained these in the Egyptian bazaar by the Galata Bridge.

It is not easy to talk to people in a capital city. They are busy and in any case it was the height of the tourist season. But while sitting in a tiny square under the shadow of the Roman aqueduct which I had just photographed, I got into conversation with a strange, half mad man. I was near a water-melon stall and its owner signalled with his eyes and a shrug that this man was odd. He sat beside me under the shade of a tree and began a conversation in Turkish, none of which I could follow. At first I thought he wanted money – he had all the appearance of a typical beggar – and I made the mistake of offering him some. He was outraged and I hastily apologised. Then he continued talking and in the end wished me luck – I think – before he ambled away. The water-melon man then made some remark and treated me to a slice of his wares.

I had been trying to learn at east some elementary Turkish from a Turkish phrase book for months before my arrival but I confess that I did not find the language easy. In Istanbul there was no real problem; plenty of people spoke English or German and I could get by without difficulty. I wondered, though, about how I could progress later.

I booked a passage on the *Truva*, one of the passenger steamships which ply back and forth the length of Turkey's Black Sea coast, though I could only obtain a deck passage. I decided to go to Ordu which was the point where the ship stopped beyond Bafra, where my journey proper would begin. The *Truva* set sail in the evening so I spent the afternoon repacking and arranging my old army backpack. Then I went down to the small hotel lounge and had some tea to fill in the time before my departure. I had put on my skywalker boots, suitable for walking and climbing, and these attracted great attention from two Turks in the hotel.

'You do not need such boots for Istanbul' one said in the astonished way curious people adopt when they mean to obtain an answer.

'I am leaving Istanbul this evening' I replied. 'Oh,' he intoned 'and which way will you be going – to Mount Ararat?' It was a fair try so I told him of my planned journey along the Kizil Irmak and he became very excited. He assured me that it was a marvellous idea, which certainly made me feel good just before I set out.

I took a taxi to the waterfront. I had been warned to bargain for the price beforehand but had forgotten. The hotel receptionist had suggested that a fair price would be about TL 1,000 but the driver took me a long way round and demanded TL 15,000, twice what I had been charged from the airport. I refused and we had a haggle. In the end I gave him TL 3,000. He pretended outrage then laughed and drove off with a wave.

I found myself a reasonable corner on the upper deck of the packed ship, and began to exercise my limited German upon a Turk. I became friends with a young Danish couple who had settled upon deck-space near to mine. We sailed down the Bosporus to the Black Sea as the sun set, revealing the Istanbul skyline in all its glory. I was two nights and a day on the *Truva*, which stopped at Zonguldak and Sinop before reaching Ordu. I enjoyed sleeping under the stars, something I had not done for ages, and lazed the day away watching the hazy coastline that had been hugged by the Argonauts of legend.

The day became increasingly hot, the decks were littered with sunbathers and only the wind created by our speed made the heat bearable. I ate fruit which I had brought with me for the journey – grapes and peaches – and drank water. My Danish friends had a bottle of whisky which provided us with nightcaps. Lazing on that deck I found how quickly time can change: without the daily compulsions of working, time became quite different and it seemed far longer than five days since I had left London. A middle-aged English couple came to sit in my part of the deck. The woman had one of those long intelligent English faces and wore a floppy hat of a style reminiscent of the 1930s. We smiled at one another but did not speak.

We reached Sinop in the dark of the second evening and a majority of the passengers disembarked. I thought of leaving the ship too since Sinop is nearer to Bafra than Ordu but decided against doing so as the town would be crowded with tourists all seeking accommodation. Half the population, or so it seemed, had promenaded on the jetty to watch the *Truva* and her passengers but only a few people from the crowd joined the ship for the last lap to Ordu. A remark of Bo, the young Danish man, was to remain with me. He said: ' Photography is tourism.' We collect records to show we have done something and think that that is enough but as a rule we have done very little. I wanted more than just records, though I had nothing particular in mind.

As a young man I had taken an expedition into the interior of the

Borneo jungle. Immense detailed planning had gone into that project – now I had almost no plans at all. I was on my own carrying everything I should need. I did not intend any major exploration nor did I expect to be in any especially wild places. I simply *did not know* and the not knowing, the resistance to planning would, I hoped, provide half the enjoyment.

# 3

# Samsun and Advice

We reached Ordu at nine in the morning. I walked along the jetty in the company of my two Danish friends, wondering how far we would have to go to find the bus station. The Danes wanted to go to Unye which was another coast town between Ordu and Samsun. Near the end of the jetty we came upon a group of policemen. One spoke German and I asked him about buses. He directed us to a second group of policemen, one of whom turned out to speak better German – or rather to understand my German better than had the previous police-man – and we began a conversation in which he welcomed the three of us to Turkey. We did not need to worry about buses, he insisted, one would soon come. One came almost at once and our police friend ran towards the road waving his arms and blowing his whistle but he was too late. The big bus raced past the end of the jetty before he could get on to the road. 'Do not worry,' he reassured us, 'another will come soon.' So we continued our conversation, but only for a few minutes. Another Samsun bus came and this time the policeman stood magnificently in the centre of the road and brought it to a halt. Grandly he told the driver to take us on board and after thanking him for his help the three of us entered the bus to be seated at the back by a friendly man who spoke some English and turned out to be an off-duty bus driver. It was 160 kilometres (100 miles) to Samsun and 40 (25 miles) to Unye. I am not an admirer of police systems generally but I thought of the recent intervention on our behalf as an efficient and sensible use of police power.

Turkey's long-distance buses are fast, on time, comfortable and well managed. It is possible to book a place to most parts of the country and buses run every day to large towns. They are air-conditioned and the assistant to the driver – I would not exactly describe him as a conductor – comes round with fresh bottled water, sometimes biscuits and periodically, when it is hot, with a bottle of scent or eau-de-cologne which he sprinkles on the passengers' hands so that they can rub their faces with it. The effect is cooling and pleasant.

The three of us had a slow conversation with the off-duty driver until the Danish couple departed at Unye. The Turkish driver, Yakup by name, now turned his whole attention to me and began to cross-examine me, politely, as to why I had come to Turkey. The road we took hugs the coast and rises up and down, often in spectacular fashion and almost always in sight of the Black Sea. This was very blue under the bright sun.

We reached Samsun at lunchtime and Yakup invited me to eat with him. After leaving the bus, which had turned into a large terminal, we crossed the busy main road by a footbridge and then picked up a minibus or *dolmus*. This took us about a mile further along the road and then we walked past a large mosque into the old centre of town. I followed Yakup who went at speed, and though I was carrying my pack and two small bags he never offered to carry one of these. I noticed a total reluctance to offer to carry anything on the part of other friendly Turks whom I met later – to do so would be an indignity. We went into a tiny café – a workman's café it would be in England but in Turkey it was an everyman's café – where we had soup. Then we went up to the glass-fronted counter to choose our next course, a practice I followed and enjoyed throughout Turkey. I had some mutton stew.

This was my first experience of one of these small cafés. As a rule the food was excellent: at least it was tasty, cheap and filling. There was always an abundance of fresh bread on the tables and water to drink. They served Fanta or Coke but never anything stronger and sometimes only a main course – stew or kebab – would be available, though generally they also served yoghurt or *ayran* (a milky yoghurt drink) and fruit: grapes, melon or water-melon, depending upon the season. Water pitchers stood on every table and the coldness of the water and frequency with which it was changed provided a test by which the café could be graded.

When we had finished Yakup asked if I would like some tea and then led me off across a little square and down a narrow road of small shops to one where he had some friends. It was an educational supply shop whose bald, moustached proprietor, looked like the actor who plays Sarim Bey in *From Russia with Love*. Everyone in the shop was engaged dispatching orders and with Yakup and myself there were never less than six people crowded into it.

The proprietor, several of his staff and various neighbours, customers or friends who kept dropping in, each wished to question me – I had begun to grow a beard on the *Truva* and my appearance at once attracted attention – but we could not understand one another since Yakup's English was strictly limited and we made little progress until someone thought to send for a young man who spoke English. He had spent some time in Northampton learning the shoe business and was happy to act as interpreter.

Everyone was intrigued by my plan to go up the Kizil Irmak and each gave contradictory advice, or so at least it seemed in the fast-talking, friendly atmosphere of the shop. A boy brought a tray of the little glasses of tea which were handed round: he was to be kept busy by us for the next two hours. They pored over my map which we spread out on a pile of primary text-books and then someone remembered the barrage. A great dam was being constructed at Kolay, upstream from Bafra, and so I would not be able to keep to the river at all, they told me. This was an unexpected set-back. More tea was brought. They said I would have to get permission from the construction company if I wished to go upriver, past the dam. A small map that showed where the water would rise and which villages had disappeared was now brought out for my benefit and it did begin to look as though I would face real problems in the early part of my journey.

Yakup now had to leave but he had arranged a lift to Bafra for me in the truck which was to take educational supplies to Sinop that afternoon. Yakup was the first of many Turks who gave me hospitality and came to my assistance in other ways. When he had to go he ensured that others took on the responsibility of helping the stranger. His was part of a recurring pattern of behaviour which I encountered all over Turkey. As a rule the only return demanded of me was information; all my hosts and helpers wished to satisfy their curiosity about me. It was a fair exchange.

Hussein, the shop's owner, now took me to his nearby warehouse where the truck was being loaded for Sinop. He produced an exceedingly sharp knife from somewhere and excused himself: he just had to go out to the back and kill a sheep, he told me. There was a feast that he and his family were about to celebrate. So I sat on a little stool in the busy street. This time another boy brought glasses of cool lemon for us to drink; it was a hot, still day and I watched the street scene. Plastic bags of sheep's entrails were now brought from behind the warehouse where the killing had taken place and my host returned looking pleased with himself. He produced another map and once more I went over my proposed route with him and a new group of his cronies who wished to question me all over again. Hussein also produced a small English-Turkish dictionary for me. This was to prove far more valuable than my Turkish phrase-book.

At last the truck was ready to leave – it was then about four in the afternoon – and after goodbyes I climbed aboard and we were off. Bafra is about 50 kilometres (31 miles) from Samsun but we stopped twice on the way, for petrol and then to deliver something at a holiday camp on the seashore. Bafra is about 20 kilometres inland on the banks of the Kizil Irmak, for silt brought down by the river over many centuries has built up an extended headland of flat rich black soils.

My first sight of the Kizil Irmak was a disappointment. We crossed it by a bridge and beyond that one road went south along the river bank to Kolay and the site of the dam which we had discussed for half the afternoon. At this point the Kizil Irmak meandered within its broad bed, but half of this was dry, the river little more than a shallow stream, an unimpressive end to a 1,290-kilometre (800-mile) journey. I had expected something a good deal more grand and imposing. The driver took me into the centre of town and I gave him a packet of English cigarettes – the only present people were more than happy to accept. My supplies would not last very long.

I got a room in the Trabzon Hotel in the centre of town, where I appeared to be the only guest. My room was spartan but clean; there was a separate, locked bathroom at the end of the corridor. I had a shower and then set out to explore the town. It was extremely hot and even wandering through its busy streets and the market I soon found myself to be perspiring freely. I am in my fifties and the subject of my age had cropped up twice that day. In the bus from Ordu Bo had turned courteously to me after some conversation with Yakup to explain that he had referred to me as the older man. Did I mind? Hardly! Then in the shop one of them had asked me how old I was. I asked what he thought – he was a young man – and he replied that his friend thought I was in my fifties but he thought I was 60!

I had my supper in the *Restoran Hacibaba* and sat on a balcony overlooking a small square. It was an excellent meal and I finished with a *raqi*, a drink I came to appreciate. *Raqi* is normally taken with water: half a glass of *raqi* is topped up with water so that the drink turns a milky white while a second glass of water and a plate of fruit – grapes, sliced peaches or melon – accompany it. One takes a sip of *raqi*, then one of water, followed by a grape or slice of melon. It is a pleasant way to take a strong drink and as I sat on that balcony I felt that my real journey was about to begin.

# 4

# The Black Sea

Before heading upstream I decided to take a day to walk from Bafra along the Kizil Irmak to its mouth on the Black Sea. The silt from the river has distorted the coast into a V-shaped headland and Bafra and the main road lie about 20 kilometres (12 miles) inland. It would be an easy first walk especially as I would only take my shoulder-bag although, as I came to discover in the following weeks, that could be quite heavy. In it I carried my camera and film, a spare lens, money, passport, notebook and map. The night before I had purchased a melon and a loaf of bread and with my water-bottle these made quite a weight. Kosukoy was the name of the village nearest the headland and I set out on the Kosukoy road at seven-thirty that morning.

I made good progress for the first hour and a half. The day was still cool and the road flat. It was rich farming country – the many tractors I met along the way testified to that – and I passed one farm after another. Everyone I encountered, whether driving tractors, the ubiquitous little minibuses, or on foot, stared their amazement at my appearance. It was perfectly clear that foreigners were simply not seen walking as I was then doing. I did not mind the stares and greeted people with 'Merhaba', the Turkish hello. For the first part of my walk there were farms between me and the river and I was only able to sit on its bank for the first time at about ten o'clock. My feet hurt!

Later I passed a large group of people who were preparing to have a picnic among the trees to one side of the road. It was a Sunday and they were in holiday mood. Already there was music – the reedy notes of a flute were accompanied by a constant, vibrant drumbeat – and there was much laughter and shouting. When I thought I had left them behind I sat on a log and ate half my melon. The day had become much hotter and I was thirsty. But three men from the picnic group had followed me and now appeared out of the trees behind me. We exchanged greetings and they sat round to talk or, as I was soon to

14

think of such occasions, to inquire. Language proved a major barrier but not for long; a teenage boy drifted up, was given instructions and promptly dispatched, to return almost immediately accompanied by a much younger boy but one who spoke very passable English. This pattern was to be repeated many times on my journey: schoolboys were constantly requisitioned to act as interpreters.

There is a fine balance between friendly courtesy to a stranger and inquisitiveness – 'Turks are curious' my London informant had told me – and the Turks are adept at mixing the two. The genuine warmth of the welcome makes subsequent resistance to inquiry difficult to maintain without the appearance of boorishness. None the less, it took me a while to accustom myself to the constant questioning to which I was subjected from this point onwards. This was one of the first occasions that I was obliged to submit to an inquisition. The three men asked the questions while the boy interpreted: where did I come from; what was my country; what did I do for a living; where was I going; why had I come to Turkey; did I like Turkey; why was I walking; what was the point of following the Kizil Irmak? When they had exhausted the immediate questions – I have no doubt they would have come up with others – they invited me to join their party in the trees but I declined. I wanted to get to the Black Sea. They said it was another 5 or 6 kilometres (3 or 4 miles), we shook hands and I set off walking again.

The country now opened out into almost parklike grassland until I came to Kosukoy. There was a tea house on the edge of the small village and I stopped for a drink before walking the final distance to the sea – as yet there was no sign of water. The tea-house had a full complement of men, never women, and several men came over to my table to greet me and ask questions. One spoke a little German, enough to enable him to find out where I came from and where I was going. He relayed this information to the room at large. I had two glasses of tea but when I went to pay the proprietor refused to take any money: my drinks were on the house.

There is a small undistinguished lighthouse standing in the sand and scrubby grass to mark the headland, Bafra Point, where the Kizil Irmak flows into the Black Sea. The heat was now unrelenting, the sea calm as a millpond and brilliant blue, the beach of white sand fringed by large tufts of coarse grass which cut the skin. The dry sand above the high-water mark was so hot that it burnt my feet. I had a long slow swim. All this time there was no sign of any other human being but now a tractor and trailer came along the path I had followed, bringing a group of young men to break the peace. They greeted me and then went to bathe while I walked to the point where the Kizil Irmak finally meets the Black Sea.

Back in the village I had more tea and discovered that a minibus left for Bafra in half an hour. The same men who had been there two hours earlier all appeared to be in place as permanent fixtures. They greeted me but since I had already been questioned they then left me alone. This was one of the more disconcerting aspects of Turkish curiosity. Once a stranger, me in this case, had been questioned and had answered to the satisfaction of his interrogators they then ignored him as of no further interest.

I calculated that altogether I had walked about 25 kilometres (15 miles). The *dolmus* kept stopping to pick up passengers who went for 2 or 3 kilometres (1 or 2 miles) only, and a young man who spoke French interpreted my answers to the rest of the passengers' questions: 'What was I doing, where did I come from . . . ?' That evening I returned to the *Restoran Hacibaba* for my supper to be greeted by the proprietor with obvious pleasure. At the end of my meal in appreciation of my patronage he came to drink a glass of *raqi* with me.

# 5

# The Dam

The next morning I took a *dolmus* to Kolay. My critics might argue that this was a poor start to a journey in which I proposed to walk along the Kizil Irmak but the road from Bafra along the left bank of the river appeared dusty and heavy with traffic to the dam site and in any case I wanted to get clear of construction complications and into my real journey as soon as possible. The distance from Bafra to Kolay was 23 kilometres (14 miles) – less than half an hour by *dolmus* – and I had been told that the company headquarters of the builders were in Kolay, though my informant was somewhat doubtful.

We kept close to the river bank and almost at once the land began to rise steeply. The maps show hills with heights of 1100 or more metres (3,600 feet) and this indeed was the case: a wall of hills the height of Wales' highest mountain, Snowdon, rises almost vertically from the coast. The Kizil Irmak valley closed in upon us and the *dolmus* reached the little village of Kolay. I was the only person to alight; the other passengers – all men – were going to the site to seek work.

In the village square I found myself the immediate centre of attention. I said *chai* (tea) meaning a tea-house but they laughed and instead of answering found someone who spoke German. I asked about company headquarters. I had made a mistake. There was nothing to do with the dam in Kolay. I would have to travel a further 10 kilometres (6 miles) to the dam site. A friendly man with no German or English signalled he would take me and led me to a stationary *dolmus*. I was his sole passenger and we set off for the dam.

I had not smoked cigarettes for 18 years but I took up the practice again in Turkey. I did so for social reasons. I found that almost everyone smoked and constantly offered me cigarettes. More important from my point of view, a cigarette was about the only thing I could offer that would be accepted in return for help or hospitality. I had brought my duty-free ration of cigarettes – Benson and Hedges – with me and these proved immensely popular whenever I offered them. I, however, smoked *Samsun*, one of the cheap local brands which I was normally offered. I began smoking warily, not inhaling, and hoped not to become an addict again. When I had given up smoking years before my daily consumption had been between 60 and 80.

The driver picked up a man at the roadside who spoke some German and I then took part in a three-sided conversation as he questioned me about my intentions. The backpack intrigued them: did I really mean to walk? Both accepted a cigarette.

The dam was an impressive sight. Its huge wall rose 152 metres (500 feet), a massive barrier across the steep-sided valley. My driver took us to a hut where he got instructions; then we continued across the great construction site up a steep dirty road to a complex of huts which housed the works foremen and engineers. The consultants were Japanese.

My driver had to go. He refused any payment for his help, asked if I was happy to be left and drove off. A young Japanese engineer or consultant asked me in good English what I wanted. I told him I was simply passing through and wished to follow the river beyond the dam. He raised a Japanese eyebrow, smiled courteously and said what an interesting idea it was. Then he shook my hand and excused himself; he had to go to work. When he had departed the Turkish foremen – at least that is what I assumed them to be – invited me into a small office. 'Tea?' they asked, and it was at once made. I had two glasses in quick succession and this was clearly a mark in my favour. 'The Japanese', they said, 'only ever take one glass. They do not think they should have two glasses with us.' He shrugged eloquently. One of the men spoke quite good English and slowly, as I explained, he informed the others of what I had in mind. Then the three Turks had a debate as to which side of the river I should take. At first everyone favoured the left bank. I looked across the dam site to the almost sheer hills, here quite thickly covered in trees but with no visible sign of road, track or village. When I pointed this out they assured me that a village was not far off. They pointed vaguely upriver. 'You cannot miss the path', they told me.

'Breakfast?' they inquired and a plate of bread, olives, goat's milk cheese and a kind of damson jam was produced. More tea was made.

'My friend here', the English-speaker said, indicating a second man who had no English, 'comes from this part. You must go across to the other side of the river. That is the best way, he says.' I nodded, busy with olives and goat's cheese. The other man then excused himself; he had to go to work. We shook hands and I was left with my English-speaking host who appeared to be the senior Turk on the site, and a second man. There was also a boy who made the tea.

The second man now talked volubly in Turkish; a problem had clearly arisen. After a while the interpreter told me that this other man insisted I should take the near side of the river. It was easier walking and the authorities were cutting a new road to the high villages now that the old roads alongside the river had been submerged by the rising waters of the dam lake. We left the hut to peer up the harsh, steep hillside. The second man pointed and talked, the first one translated: 'That road leads to the village of Akalan. There are other villages along the way. You will come across government road workers. There will be no problem.' After some further debate I decided to take the near – right-hand – side of the river.

It was now that my host, Muhurrem Koc, said he would write a letter for me: 'It will help you in the villages', he said. So he proceeded laboriously to write a letter in Turkish which I was to find had varying results depending upon its readers. It translated into English as follows:

Good day,
This gentleman is an English subject as I understand. He has an intention to reach Osmancik from Bafra by walking. To reach to his aim he needs your help. I am sure that whoever you are you will show our traditional hospitality and I am sure you will help him. He is the guest of our country and in the village all the concerned people should help him to meet his needs. He wants to find out how the people live in Turkish villages. He has no other aim. His only aim is to find out the living conditions of the Turkish village as close as possible. On his behalf we thank you very much for your help beforehand.

PS I (the author) make several studies of different countries and their living style of the world and I am going to publish this research. I hope in the near future I will publish my research about Turkey and Turkish people.

Muhurrem was no scholar but his missive was certainly to prove of great interest to a number of subsequent readers. The PS was his paraphrase of part of our conversation. I felt that I had been supplied with a Sultan's *firman* (permit) as of old.

I filled my water-bottle with fresh water, shook hands all round and then set off up a steep, wide, newly-graded road. It was then eleven in the morning and hot, with the clear intention of getting much hotter. After 1 kilometre (three quarters of a mile) winding and rising steadily I came to a platform overlooking the dam and lake below. There was an awning over the platform on which two men sat drinking tea. They invited me to take a glass with them and informed me I had come the wrong way. This was a dead end, the platform merely an observation post from which to see that all was well with the dam below. Gratefully I drank tea, perspiring freely after my first 20 minutes of walking. A lovely breeze wafted across the valley. Already we were 90 metres (300 feet) above the dam, so steeply had my path risen. The waters of the lake had reached two thirds of the way up the dam wall, while the lake snaked back out of sight between the steep hills of what must have been an awesome gorge. Now I understood why the river between Bafra and the sea had seemed such a miserable trickle.

I had to descend the hill and begin again. I came to another path junction and this time took the left fork. I rose steeply into another dead end, a stone quarry for the dam. It was getting much hotter and this was not an auspicious beginning. Finally I got on to the correct path – the only one left for me to take – and began a slow trudge up into the hills. The sun beat down mercilessly and I began to remember my age. Whenever I came to convenient shade under a tree at the edge of the path I rested, finding that I needed those rests. By one o'clock I decided to rest properly and arranged my groundsheet on the side of the road right against the sheer rock face which now provided about 30 cm (1 foot) of shade. Instantly I fell asleep. I came wide awake to find a young man standing beside me. Unlike me he had no pack to carry but was still sweating from the effort of the climb. I offered him my water-bottle but he refused with a courteous gesture, asked whether I was all right and then continued walking up the hill. I slept a while longer before resuming my slow upward march. The heat had become even more oppressive.

Perhaps 3 kilometres (2 miles) further on I came upon a huge yellow caterpillar excavator at the roadside, its crew resting in its shade to drink tea. They eyed me with astonishment and invited me to join them. This I was happy to do. I had had practically nothing since my breakfast of cheese and olives at the dam site and that tea was one of the best drinks of any kind I can ever remember. There were three men and a boy whose sole function as far as I could see was to carry things and make tea. He was now sent off to a nearby stream to refill the kettle. One of the men spoke some German and after a halting conversation I remembered Muhurrem's letter. This was a good opportunity to see what effect it produced. I handed it to the man who appeared to be the foreman of the group, and he read it out to the others. Then we retreated up the bank to some green grass 6 metres (20 feet) above the road and settled down for a rest while the 'foreman' took the great excavator and tackled a bank further down the steep dirt road. For an hour he cut and banked and smoothed the earth, the alternating roar and hum of his machine providing a soothing background for the rest of us. We smoked, talked occasionally and moved to keep in the shade of a solitary tree. The first driver stopped the machine and changed places with the second man, and the work continued. I am not sure what the third man did: he was not a driver. At five o'clock the machine was turned off. The foreman offered me a bed for the night in his working caravan which I had passed before I reached them but the man who did not drive – the least important of the trio – had already invited me to be his guest in the village, an invitation I had accepted, so I now shouldered my pack and set off up the hill with my host and the tea boy.

# 6

# Village Hospitality

Leaving the two drivers at the caravan I set off with my host and the tea boy along the newly-cut road. This continued to rise steadily. Now, far below us, the long lake of the dam meandered like a huge fat snake which bulged in odd places; its waters were difficult to distinguish in the heat haze and the day's fierce temperature had only just begun to abate. The new dirt road they were constructing did not go much further and soon we were walking along a track in the outskirts of Akalan. The tea boy left us to seek his own home while we continued into the centre of the village, which must have been at a height of about 1,065 metres (3,500 feet) with a dramatic view across the deep Kizil Irmak valley. Somewhere far below but now out of sight was the river lake which stretched back some 60 kilometres (40 miles) through the hills from the great dam. The houses of Akalan were scattered among undulating hills and in the gardens of almost every one of them were 'clothes'-lines of tobacco leaves which had been hung out in close formation, the leaves tightly packed against each other, to cure in the sun. Bafra District is the centre of Turkish tobacco growing.

My host's house was at the beginning of the densest part of the village although there was a fine long-distance view from the porch. I removed my boots and entered. His wife, apparently in her fifties, though she may have been younger, greeted me but did not offer to shake hands. This, I discovered, was normal custom. She had a stern, strong face and rarely smiled. My host at once took me upstairs into the best room and invited me to leave my pack there. Then we returned down the steep wooden stairs to the 'hall' in front of the kitchen where his wife was busy preparing food, helped by one of her teenage daughters. Almost at once she produced a meal. She placed a large round tray in front of her husband and myself as we sat cross-legged on the floor. On it was a substantial omelette, a bowl of yoghurt and bread. We each had a fork and spoon and helped ourselves alternately from the omelette and yoghurt. Once the two of us had slowed our eating pace – though we had certainly not given up – other members of the family sat round to eat with us. There were two teenage girls, one of them quite exceptionally pretty, and two boys of about eleven and nine.

The wife now joined our circle round the table and questioned my host about me, glancing at me each time he answered one of her queries. There was a sort of slow determination about her; she was going to find out all he knew abut me, which was not much, and then, I suspected, some more on her own account. After a while the girls and one of the boys excused themselves although the younger boy – his father's favourite – stayed and his mother now produced tea. I always enjoyed watching the preparations for tea: the samovar would be set boiling, the glasses produced and carefully wiped, a bowl of sugar placed nearby. This was an old samovar and she put small pieces of burning wood from the range fire into it until the sound of bubbling told us the tea would soon be ready. I enjoy tea anyway, which is a good thing if you travel in Turkey. Now I was to become accustomed to drinking endless small glasses of samovar tea until there was none left. My host was assiduous in refilling my glass, clearly delighted that I enjoyed it so much. While we were drinking tea I congratulated the stern mother on her lovely children, mainly in sign language, and when she was sure she understood what I meant she permitted herself a rare smile. It was a smile of deep contentment; she was fulfilled and happy. Physically she showed the signs of having lived an incredibly hard life: her hands were big like a man's and calloused from work, her face lined and old before its time, her figure had lost most of its shape. But her children were lovely and my reference to them brought both pride and joy into her face. Then my host invited me to sit on the porch.

Although I had not walked very far in distance that day it certainly seemed as though I had. It had been exceptionally hot, it was my first day with my pack and I had had to rise very steeply into the hills. As a result I felt exhausted. My host, whose courtesy would shame many more sophisticated people, realised that I just wanted to rest a while so he excused himself and left me propped against one of the log rails of the porch. I watched the village street immediately below the porch and a steep path which rose sharply above the house on its other side. The street was narrow and dusty, now composed of soft dry earth which must have become a muddy slipway in rain or snow. Almost all the people who came past the house were women: driving hens or geese, leading a donkey, carrying heavy loads. They certainly appeared to do all the work around the village, but then few men were in sight. All the women wore headscarves and most of them covered their mouths when they saw me.

My host and I talked in sign language though I kept referring to my phrase-book. He would say something in Turkish which I did not understand;. I would reply in English which he did not understand. I would make vague hand gestures to which he would reply in kind. Then I would resort to my Turkish phrase-book. Finally both of us would sit back and laugh, exhausted by this frustrating intellectual effort. We would try again. I then thought of drawing things, and this did work sometimes – later when I wanted to ask about the possibility of hiring a donkey I drew what with me passes for a donkey, though my drawing skills look like those of a backward child of four or five who is averse to drawing anyway. I produced a vague likeness to a donkey with a pack on its back, a boy leading it and me walking behind. This produced a dramatic response of hilarious understanding laughter – it did not produce a donkey. This first major conversation took place after I had been allowed half an hour on the porch by myself to rest. Then my host suggested I might like to take a walk with him round the village.

I was a prized possession and he wanted to show me off to the other men in the village. Unfortunately no one appeared to be back from their day's activities and my host's face became longer and longer. We did meet an awkward young man leading two donkeys with immense piles of hay heaped on their backs. He was the village idiot and guffawed his amazement at the sight of me to the embarrassment of my host who told him sharply to be about his business. We picked up a cloth bag someone had dropped and hung it on a convenient tree so that its owner would find it again. Then we returned to the house. I was not in training and the day's walking, slow and interrupted though it had been, had left me exhausted. All I wanted to do was go to bed.

It was almost dark when we got back to the house and now my host led me up to the best room. This was bare of furniture except for a built-up divan the length of one wall, which was covered with rugs and small cushions. He motioned me to sit on it. A thick carpet covered the floor and several tapestries hung on the walls. We sat, making slow 'gesture' conversation – my host was almost as tired as I – and for a while no one else came into the room. I tried to keep my eyes open and wondered what would happen next. My host would say something, smile and nod. I would do likewise and then we would lapse into silence again. This went on for some time. Then, at about nine o'clock things began to happen.

The wife and daughters now entered. They set a large flat wooden drum like the frame of a garden sieve in the centre of the floor, covered it with a cloth and then placed an enormous round brass tray on top of it to make a table. They then brought in a number of dishes: different beans, cucumber yoghurt, stewed meat. The fare was simple but appealing and I began to come alive again. My host signalled to me to take my place beside the tray, and sitting cross-legged on the floor I copied him: I raised the nearest piece of the table-cloth which had been draped over the wooden drum and spread this over my lap. Then we ate. Meanwhile one of the daughters had brought in the samovar and fresh tea was made. And then the guests arrived.

The men I had not seen on my walk round the village with my host had none the less materialised. Word of my presence had got round and curiosity had to be satisfied. Some dropped in for a brief stay, shook hands with me, had a glass of tea and then left. Others settled comfortably, cross-legged on the rugs, ready for a long session. We would hear someone come up the steep wooden stairs and then, gently, he would push open the door and peer into our brightly-lit room to offer a greeting, but wait to be invited to join us. My host – I never did discover his name – was in his element. He introduced me, he ordered his daughters or one of the several teenage boys to deal with the samovar, he handed round grapes. I discovered that my map was of immense help in place of language. I could indicate without much difficulty where I had come from and where I intended to go. Istanbul would be found and imitations of aeroplanes would demonstrate how I had got there from England.

The only other piece of furniture in the room which I had not taken in – it was draped with a rug in the corner – turned out to be a large television set. For half an hour my host fiddled with wire connections, and awful wavering half pictures flickered on and off. It was his new toy and he longed to demonstrate it to everybody but the reception was so bad that in the end he was obliged to give up. Meanwhile everyone had been concentrating upon my map.

One of the penalties of being a guest in a peasant society is that you are, as it were, up for inspection. Tired though I was I had to keep at my best and brightest, willing to be inspected and ready to answer questions. I revived at the sheer courtesy of the process. They showed such pleasure in my presence amongst them that it was impossible to resent the endless sometimes almost inquisitorial questioning that went on for three hours. Part of the trouble was that I had to keep repeating myself: just when I had completed an explanation of my intentions a newcomer would arrive and his curiosity had to be satisfied anew. Three hours of conversation conducted entirely by signs, phrase-book or gestures can be exhausting.

An exceptionally old man sat in the exact centre of the room – I was cross-legged on the divan like a vizier in his court – who was both the object of jokes and the recipient of respect at the same time. He had blood-rimmed eyes which bulged from a face lined with tiny, purple blood-vessels. He turned these prominent eyes with a quick gesture towards those who joked at him and whenever he did so raised a laugh. He produced a 23-cm (9-inch) long elaborately carved wooden cigarette-holder and puffed with great concentration as though it were a pipe, and periodically, after maintaining calculated silences, he made remarks – in his day I suspect he had been the village wit – which caused delayed laughter for their impact was not always at once apparent.

At last around midnight everyone left. Then my host opened a carved door in the wall – he told me that he had carved it himself – and took blankets and pillows from a cupboard. He arranged these on the divan for me, took me to see the lavatory, made certain I wanted for nothing then shook hands and closed the door on me for the night, joining his wife in their room at the back of the house. I fell asleep to the fading night sounds of the village.

# 7

# Through the Hills by Donkey

The night was cool and I awoke at five in the morning feeling marvellously rested. In the still deep silence of early dawn I sat on the broad window-sill to write my notes as the slow first light of a yet invisible sun brought the distant hills to life. Then the village came hiccuping awake. A cock crowed. A dog barked to be promptly answered by a second dog from the other side of the village. Someone stirred, decided it was too early and became quiet again, but not for long. Soon came the unmistakable sounds of a community rousing itself. I could hear the family getting up. Then my host tapped on my door and came in. We shook hands and he sat with me. Since we were without benefit of interpreter conversation was strictly limited. He would sit silent for a while and then make a remark in Turkish; I would reply in English. We would look at each other and laugh, then lapse once more into silence. He was a man of wonderful courtesy and easiness. Despite a lack of communication I had absolutely no sense of awkwardness with him. He was a peasant of little education; he was also one of the finest hosts ever to entertain me.

Tea and then a breakfast of soup and hard-boiled eggs and freshly-made unleavened bread and yoghurt set me up for the coming day's walk. My host's wife permitted herself a smile when her four children had assembled round the tray of breakfast food and I had greeted each in turn. When she did smile her face, fleetingly, revealed a hint of the beauty she must have possessed as a young woman.

I set off just after seven and my host came to make sure I took the correct path out of the village. We passed the cloth bag which he had hung on a tree the night before so that its owner would find it easily, and when I pointed to it he laughed and nodded his pleasure that we had put it there. At the edge of the village he indicated the track I should take. This wound its way across an open hill and into the forest. We shook hands and I set off. I looked back after 50 metres. He was

27

still standing there and I waved. Then he turned back into the village and I concentrated upon the path ahead of me.

The morning was cool and overcast and I hoped it would remain so. The path wound through high forest and whenever I came to a break in the trees it was only to see more forest across the valley. A lone dog appeared on the path ahead of me to bark furiously at my approach but he slipped into the trees to let me pass. I walked for about an hour before taking a rest where a break in the trees afforded a magnificent view up the great valley which stretched for miles far below me. I could see nothing of the lake and was not at all certain whether I was following the Kizil Irmak or some other valley, for I had been twisting steadily along the forest path.

I heard them for some time before they came into sight along the track: a small man sitting astride a donkey and a boy leading it. We exchanged greetings and the man promptly got off his donkey to sit beside me. We looked over the great valley, still coloured the misty blue of early morning. Then I offered him one of my English cigarettes. His eyes lit up and he made clear signs that he would buy the whole pack: what did I want for them? I refused his offer and gave him the pack instead. He was delighted and put his treasure carefully away. Then he offered to carry my pack on the donkey. This suited me so we fixed it on the wooden saddle and set off – the boy leading the donkey, the man walking behind with a stick with which he gave the beast an occasional crack across the rump, while I brought up the rear. Nuri was a small, engaging character and sang as he walked. The boy, who was about eleven, was his son.

We continued through deep forest and I would surely have lost that path on my own. It had dwindled to almost nothing and more than once we had to negotiate fallen trees. We came out on to a high open place, then dropped right down to the valley bottom, or at least to a steep-sided little valley with a stream rushing through it. This was not the main valley. Under an overhanging rock Nuri pointed to a huge dog: it was in its death-throes and lay slowly panting out its last. Then our path rose steeply again. The boy leading the donkey never paused; his father sang and laughed, sometimes throwing his arms wide with pleasure at the hills and then turning to share his enjoyment with me while I followed, panting, woefully out of training.

We came on to the spur of a great hill where the forest gave way to open rough pastureland and then fields. There was a village beyond and Nuri said that he knew people there and we would stop for a rest – and a visit. The village was still some way off and we paused while

I took a photograph of Nuri, his son and the donkey. Then we continued into the village.

Elalan was perched on sharp eminences so that its dirt roads wound steeply up and down, one house overlooking the roof of its neighbour. We came to a house where an old, thick vine had been trained over a trellis across the path to provide a wonderfully cool, sheltered place in the middle of the village street. Two young men, relatives of Nuri, invited us into the house, where tea was at once produced. While I drank Nuri talked about me, though what he said I could only guess at. Then food was produced and we moved into a circle round the now familiar tray. It was a substantial meal: bean soup, mutton, yoghurt, raw onions, tomatoes and unleavened bread with cold water to drink. I had developed an enormous thirst and made no concession to the warnings I had been given about drinking other than bottled spring-water. I would deal with stomach upsets or worse when they occurred.

Now we went visiting. Like my host of the night before Nuri wished to show me off. We descended to a lower part of the village where I met part of the large Bulut clan. The patriarch of this family – he was 60, he told me later – was thickset and strong, slow to smile or indeed to reveal any expression. We sat round the walls of a large barnlike room while tea was dispensed from a samovar. Newcomers would cross the room to shake hands with me then find a space against the wall of their own. I produced my letter which I passed to my host but after a brief glance he handed it to a younger man with a gesture of indifference which might have concealed a reading blockage and told him to read it out to the room. The young man complied but he had such difficulty, pausing and stumbling so often, that the rest lost interest long before he came to an end and he appeared to be reading to himself in the middle of the general conversation.

'Did I have a camera?' someone asked. He had just been talking to Nuri.

'Yes, I did.' There was a pause but I knew what was wanted. I pointed through the window indicating sunlight and as one man everyone in the room rose to his feet and trooped outside. I arranged them, the older Bulut as was his due in the centre of the group. His son, a 30-year-old replica of his father, helped arrange the group. Turks love having their photographs taken. At the sight of a camera the men straighten out their clothes, flick off real or imaginary dust, run their hands carefully through their hair, hold a discussion as to whether they should allow themselves to be taken bareheaded or with their caps on, and then they pose. I found it almost impossible to get them to be natural. They puffed out their chests, folded their arms, and stared firmly ahead with lofty expressions. They loved it. So did I, but there was a drawback. Once I had finished taking pictures they lined up to give me their names and addresses: 'Would I send copies from England when I returned?'

Nuri said we had another visit to make and once more we set off through the village. But the older Bulut was not finished with me: he wanted a packet of my English cigarettes, and came too. He was a persistent dour man with little humour, and he was not interested in me, only the cigarettes. Back at the house where I had left my things I took out a packet for him. He grabbed it, eyes gleaming, and went at once as though it had been a payment for services rendered, hardly bothering to say goodbye. I had enjoyed hospitality in his house and did not in the least begrudge the cigarettes, although my supplies were dwindling fast, but I found him less than courteous: there was a grasping quality in his attitude towards me which I met later in his son.

In a third house we sat round the best room during the heat of the afternoon; half the men lay back to sleep. I did so and someone placed a light cloth over my head to keep off the mosquitoes. I woke to the clink of glass. A samovar had been produced and everyone sat up to take tea. This was followed by food: large spring onions, hard-boiled eggs, beans, yoghurt and whey. Then Nuri signalled that it was time to go, but outside the house I took more photographs. An ancient couple, great-grandparents at least, came hobbling out, the woman bent double with arthritis. It took some time for them to be seated on a log. Then other members of the family gathered round them and I took my pictures. Finally we set off in the same order: boy, donkey, Nuri, with me bringing up the rear. I found myself a stout rough walking-stick.

On my own I should not even have discovered the path out of the village, and thereafter the track became more and more difficult to follow as we rose into the forest, well above 1,220 metres (4,000 feet). Nuri took his hat off and signalled me to do the same so that we could enjoy the breeze. I would have been both baffled and exhausted had I tried that path alone with the pack on my back. But this was on the donkey and I assumed Nuri knew where he was going. At one point Nuri had a shouted conversation with a shepherd higher up among the trees and after a while he came down to join us, so we had a rest. I had some bread and two tomatoes in my pack from the day before which I produced cutting the tomatoes in half, and we had an impromptu feast. The shepherd produced some salt. Nuri's son had a bad gash on his leg, covered with sticking plaster which he kept removing so as to show off his wound. It was a deep clean gash but so often had he removed the dressing that it would hardly stay on any more. I had some plasters with me and put on a fresh dressing for him. Nuri was pleased at this and I told his son to leave the plaster alone, though I doubted he would for long. I gave Nuri some spare plasters. Then the shepherd disappeared up his hillside into the trees and the three of us set off once more.

We rose again through rough wooded country with only occasional traces of the path, at least to my inexperienced eyes. It was by then late afternoon and Nuri now mounted the donkey on top of my pack. Then we came out of the trees and headed towards a ridge. Turning a sharp corner the donkey slipped and Nuri was thrown into the bushes. He got up, whacked the donkey and then decided to have a rest while his son took my water-bottle and disappeared down the hillside to fill it at a little stream. Shortly after that we breasted the ridge and came on to a newly-cut dirt road. Nuri pointed ahead. His own village of Golalan, he said, was about 3 kilometres (2 miles) ahead. We came to a high point on the road and there, far below, I could see the Kizil Irmak lake, still alternately bulging and thinning like a badly-made string of sausages. It must have been the better part of 900 metres (3,000 feet) below us. Then we circled a hill and descended sharply towards Golalan.

Men and women were working in the fields and to some of them Nuri shouted greetings, other he ignored; once he got off his donkey to go and talk with a man. Then we came into the village down a steep track between rocks and high banks. Nuri's house was small, in an angle of the village street, and looked both dilapidated and dirty. His wife and another woman sat outside threading tobacco leaves on thick bodkin-like needles about 35 cm (14 inches) in length. When 25 cm (10 inches) of leaves were tightly packed against each other the women would pull these down on to a long piece of twine, which would later be stretched against one of the house walls like a clothes-line for the leaves to cure. The boy disappeared, taking the donkey with him, Nuri brought me a stool to sit on in the little dirt road and then – a great privilege – produced a small cup of Turkish coffee. After that he took one of the great bodkins and sat threading tobacco leaves with the women. Men who came past greeted me and came over to shake hands, but they did not stay. Once in the village, Nuri's personality had changed. He was no longer carefree as he had been in the hills. He had now adopted the attitude of a man with responsibilities and he was certainly choosy about those villagers with whom he was prepared to talk, yet, interestingly, his house was one of the least impressive in the village. Perhaps his aloofness was a defence mechanism.

We only entered the house when it became too dark to work outside any longer; it was small and dirty with flies everywhere. We sat for a while talking and were joined by a sandy-haired man with a thin face and small, cruel mouth. He invited us to eat with his family and then left. Nuri and I threaded our way along the dirt streets in total darkness; these were often hopelessly muddy, but not from rain. Dirty water and refuse had been thrown out of the houses and in some places formed pools, in others created little rivulets which meandered down the ruts to make muddy traps for the unwary.

Our host was Hasan. There was a slyness about him which repelled. He had several small children: three boys and two girls was my count but I may well have got it wrong. The food was good and when Hasan, the older two boys, Nuri and I had eaten our fill the tray was removed to an inner room by Hasan's wife, where the women and younger children finished what remained.

Hasan asked desultory questions of me and since no one spoke either German or any English conversation was slow, largely a matter of guess-work, dependent upon the few Turkish words at my command. But I knew Hasan wanted something from me and eventually he raised his hands to his eyes and went through the motion of taking a photograph. Then he pointed to the small bag that accompanied me everywhere; in it I carried my camera and maps. I had no flash and tried to explain that a picture was unlikely to come out in such light but, I think wilfully, Hasan failed to understand me. So I took a picture of him with his boys tightly grouped round him – he was not interested in having his wife in the picture. I doubted it would be any use. Hasan then played with the boys: as far as I could see the principal object of the game was for Hasan to grasp his sons' genitals until they squealed.

We threaded our way back to Nuri's house in the dark. I was to sleep in the front room where earlier we had sat with Nuri, his son and two more children sharing the floor. We were tightly packed in the little room and, muttering her annoyance, his wife retreated to the kitchen where she had to sleep while I occupied her place in the front room. The mosquitoes now came out in force and I found I must spend the night alternately covering my head with a dirty sheet to keep them at bay or, when this became too stifling, surfacing to get some fresh air and endless mosquito bites at the same time. We settled to sleep and Nuri put out the lights, but an interruption came almost at once.

The early shufflings of a small room full of people who had not yet descended into deep sleep were still going on when Nuri was called from outside the house. He put the light on and went down the wooden steps to talk to his late visitor. Then he returned with a letter addressed in a large sprawling hand. He sat on his bedthings and everyone came to life, his wife seating herself on the floor in front of Nuri so as to follow the movement of his lips as he deciphered the letter. There was an intense family excitement which Nuri, who had an excellent sense of theatre, skilfully increased by directing each of them to settle comfortably for the reading before he would begin. The letter was from Nuri's eldest son, whose framed photograph hung on the wall above my head. This was in colour and showed a young man in soldier's uniform astride a horse. For the time being I was wholly forgotten by the family.

Slowly, in the manner of the semi-literate, Nuri spelled out the letter to his wife and children, who interrupted frequently with questions. I thought the son who had accompanied us all day wanted to take the letter from his father and read it for him – he was a bright boy – but with admirable sensitivity he restrained himself and let his father struggle on. Several times his wife laughed at what he read out so it was a happy letter. Satisfied at last – they went over every word of it laboriously twice – Nuri put out the lights and we settled down once more to sleep.

# 8

# The Road to Vezirkopru

It was a long, hard, mosquito-ridden night. I woke at five by which time the mosquitoes, sated with my blood, had become less aggressive. I lay resting until six. None of the family seemed anxious to stir so my inactivity suited the general mood, but the wife was stirring from her banishment in the kitchen and Nuri got up and went to join her. To the sounds of an animated conversation between them I then got dressed. The children covered their heads firmly with their sheets and slept on with determination. Nuri came back and told his children to get up, though only with a half-hearted authority which they ignored. Then his wife brought in the samovar and glasses.

Over tea I tried to ask Nuri whether there was any chance of a donkey and guide across the mountains to Vezirkopru. We were miles from the Kizil Irmak whose great dam lake still stretched along the deep valley and it looked as though I would have to continue in the hills for some distance before I could get back to the river again. Nuri appeared to understand but later I realised he had done no such thing. After breakfast he told me to leave my pack at his house and together we set off to visit some of his friends. I thought he would ask about a donkey but it was only to have tea. We sat outside their house looking at the hills as we drank tea and ate biscuits that had been hastily obtained from somewhere for us. Then, of course, they wanted their photographs taken. There were three men at this house – the women stayed firmly indoors – and they sat or stood solemnly while I obliged.

Later we sat in the shade of the street. A tractor came by and the two men on it stopped, exchanged greetings and asked that I should take a photograph of them sitting on their machine. I did so, beginning to realise that my expected role was to take their pictures – the men, that is – and send copies to them once back in England. I suspected that Nuri had set me up for the purpose: they were certainly very

34

prompt to give me their addresses. Time was passing, the sun was already high in the sky to give promise of an extra hot day, and I was beginning to realise that there was no likelihood of a donkey. Nuri merely wished to show me off for a while and I could hardly not oblige him after all his kindness, yet if I had to walk the sooner I left the better. Vezirkopru, I estimated, was all of 40 kilometres (25 miles) distant.

We were sitting in a strategic corner so that half the village passed us, all of whom stopped to greet me and some remained to talk. Nuri was in his element but I was getting edgy; I had a long way to go. Eventually I signalled that I must be off and with surprising alacrity Nuri agreed. We returned to his house and he fetched my pack. Then he walked with me to the steep path which rose through the cut in the rocks: 'I must keep to the road by which we had entered the village the night before; it would bring me to Vezirkopru.' We shook hands and I gave Nuri another pack of my cigarettes. Then I found myself trudging steadily upwards. It was already half past nine and hot; I had missed the best part of the walking day.

I was soon sweating profusely with the effort of that upwards toil, when two men on donkeys caught me up at an easy pace. They insisted that I rode one of the donkeys, which I did, clutching awkwardly at my pack to keep it balanced. The donkey's owner led it and me. I travelled like this for perhaps 3 kilometres (2 miles), up to the top of the ridge and for some distance along it, until they turned off into their fields. I thanked them for the lift and they shrugged as though it was of no account but I gave them some cigarettes from the pack which I had open – I was beginning to be sparing of this precious commodity – shook hands and then began walking in earnest.

I walked steadily for the next three and a half hours and despite the heat began to achieve a settled rhythm which became my norm: 5 kilometres (3 miles) an hour. I met no one. At the end of the first five kilometres (3 miles) I passed through the deserted village of Volpinar, all of whose inhabitants must have been out working in the fields for I did not see a single adult. But there were several young girls at a house on the edge of the village where the road branched. I pointed at what I thought was the main road and said 'Vezirkopru' interrogatively but they only giggled and disappeared into the house.

That dirt road appeared endless: it wound up and down over the rolling hills and I could follow its course for miles ahead of me. I saw groups of peasants, mainly women, working in the fields and once I met an old man standing on the roadside. He eyed me with astonishment. I greeted him and asked if I was on the correct road for Vezirkopru. Yes, I was, but it was a very long way, he signalled, and was I really going to walk?

By half past one I decided to rest. My water-bottle was still two thirds full but I had nothing else with me and wished to conserve its contents as long as possible. Under a small thick-leaved tree which cast just enough shadow I lay down to sleep for an hour. I had walked about 18 kilometres (11 miles) after leaving the men with the donkeys. The hill sloped away from me into a hazy distance. I had been there for about half an hour, relaxed but not sleeping, when I saw a small boy walking below me in the field carrying a large plastic water container. I hailed him but he took no notice and disappeared into the bushes. Later I saw him again and this time he looked up when I called. I made a drinking motion but he gave no response and once more disappeared into the bushes. I must have dozed for suddenly he was standing beside me holding out his plastic water container, from which I took a long drink and then another. The water was spring fresh and beautifully cold. I thanked the boy but without a word or sign he took his water container and walked off.

I began to walk again, plodding with the slow determination one adopts when faced by an apparently endless journey. If my map was accurate, which I doubted, the next village was about 10 kilometres (6 miles) away and Vezirkopru another 10 beyond that. By then it was half past three and the countryside was open, bleak, and without sign of people. Apart from the old man and the boy with the water I had met no one. Round the spur of a hill I faced a breathtaking view: endless rolling hills turning blue in the heat haze of distance and far below, swinging away from my line of march, the meandering Kizil Irmak. It was still a lake, its shores often lapping into the trees for even here the waters had risen many metres though by then it must have been 50 kilometres (30 miles) or more back from the great barrage at Kolay.

Later, when I was beginning to contemplate the possibility of a night camping out without food I heard the noise of a tractor behind me. The hum of the powerful machine came and went for a long time before it appeared at the bottom of the stretch of hill I had just climbed. It was a big yellow machine with a cabin superstructure of glass. I stood at the roadside to allow it to pass but instead it came to a halt and my friends from the village of Elalan greeted me with laughter and invited me up on to the tractor. The younger Bulut, who looked a replica of his father, was there and two others I recognised – they had all posed for the group photograph I had taken. The cabin was crowded for there were two children as well as the men and a miserable-looking hen with legs tied for market. At the back was a small trailer in which a goat was tethered; I put my pack in that – later the goat peed on it – and we set off. I offered cigarettes and they asked where I had come from that day. Conversation was not easy because of the noise of the engine and the continual bumping. I was standing, balancing, holding on to a bit of the frame and so uncomfortable that I would have preferred to be back on the road. But the tractor throbbed along at 16 kilometres (10 miles) an hour, eating up the lonely, dusty road in a way I should never have managed before nightfall. We roared through the one village that I had pinpointed on my map and shortly afterwards began a spectacular descent of the escarpment towards the broad valley where Vezirkopru lay.

Turkish farmers use their tractors as though they are also family motor cars. My friends were off to market and some celebration, they told me, hence the goat. The driver pushed his machine at speed, roaring it along the flat and then shooting up the next hill until the gradient forced him to change gear, which was exceptionally wearing on his passengers. In the approach to Vezirkopru we stopped at a bridge over a stream and got out to drink at one of the regular roadside water fountains. Then we sat on the stone coping for a rest.

After a conversation with the young Bulut, who appeared to be urging some course of action upon him, the driver turned to me – he had a little German – and indicated his tractor. After several attempts he made his point: 'Would I make a contribution to the cost of the petrol since I had had a lift from them?'

'Of course I would', but I was surprised. On various occasions I had offered, carefully, to pay for hospitality of one sort or another and usually at the merest hint my offers had been indignantly refused. I had made a firm offer to pay Nuri if he would bring his donkey and act as guide but that was different. In any case he couldn't come and I did not need a guide, only a carrier. Bulut was behind this request: when they had first picked me up he had insisted that I took his place in the tractor while he stood on the step by the great wheel, an action which in retrospect reminded me of the thieves offering the commercial traveller the couch to sleep on in Priestley's *The Good Companions*. Now he wanted payment.

The driver who had asked me was clearly embarrassed. I carried my ready money in the breast pocket of my shirt; I took out the notes that were there – about TL 6,000 – and handed these to him. He counted them, asked if that was all I had, laughed shamefacedly and then handed them back to me, got up abruptly and said we must go. So we piled into the tractor again and completed the remaining distance into Vezirkopru, where they set me down. I took the money out and said they should take it, but this time they refused adamantly: 'But you will send the photographs?' they asked. Then they drove off leaving me on the main road.

It had been a curiously difficult passage. I would have been happy enough to pay either for the lift or still more for the village hospitality but had been warned more than once about giving offence. In consequence it was always difficult to know quite what to do. My host of the first night would have been outraged had I offered to pay for his hospitality and the thought had not crossed my mind. But there was a certain hardness about the younger Bulut resembling the grasping after my cigarettes which his father had displayed.

There was a tractor garage on the edge of Vezirkopru and alongside it a tea-house. I sat on its porch and had two cold lemon drinks before making my way into the centre of town; then I found a hotel. I think it was the best one in town although my room, which included a shower (though this worked somewhat spasmodically), only cost me 2 pounds sterling. I changed and went down in search of a beer, which I was served in the dining room. Then I took out my notebook and began transposing notes into my larger, detailed diary. At once the proprietor and the barman came across, 'Was I German?' . . . English! 'Good, we Turks like the English. Mrs Tatcheer', they ended with a smile. I nodded grimly.

It was, as I discovered then and later, almost impossible to write notes in a public place. To do so was merely to advertise my foreignness and invite attention, which came quickly enough. After our first greetings I tried to continue writing.

'What do you write?'

'Notes of my journey.'

'Ah, yes. What journey is that?' So I explained. Then the barman picked up my notebook and began to examine it. 'Who is this?' He had come across Nuri's name and address, so I explained.

'That is good, to have some Turkish friends', they told me.

The proprietor then picked up the diary into which I transposed my notes. He examined the writing: 'I cannot understand this', he said.

'Good.' I replied. This response nonplussed him but not for long. Another beer was brought to me, a present from someone at the next table, where a foursome were amused spectators of my interrogation.

But after about 20 minutes my inquisitors left me — other customers needed attention — and I did get some writing done.

Later, after my evening meal, I walked into the centre of the town. It was a sultry night and outside the tea-houses the television sets would be set high, facing the street so that customers could sit in rows facing the screen while they took their tea or soft drinks or just sat talking. Turkish television, like everybody else's television, is awful, but it was lapped up with an avid attention that belied the awfulness of the product. Often, however, they were watching video melodramas. These were awful too and always followed the same pattern: macho men, women in distress, and torrid love scenes that made nonsense of the village or small-town behaviour which I invariably encountered, where the women always wore headscarves and were still in the habit of drawing these across their mouths at the sight of stranger.

# 9

# The Road to Çorum

The nature of my travelling now changed, at any rate for the time
being. Vezirkopru was not on the Kizil Irmak, for I had descended
from the hills to the east of the line of the river. I was, however, on
the main Havza to Boyabat road and this joined the river some 12
kilometres (7 miles) from Vezirkopru to run parallel with it thereafter.
For a time I was to travel along quite important roads which ran
alongside the river, and since the small towns were quite far apart I
adopted a tactic which was to serve me well. I would set myself a
target – the town or village which I had to reach that evening – and
begin walking even if it was 50 kilometres (30 miles) or more away.
Then, when I felt that I had walked enough for the day, I would take
one of the numerous *dolmus* or minibuses which plied most routes. I
might pick this up in one of the small places through which I passed,
although it was often just as easy to stand at the roadside when one
was coming; they were always looking for business. Things did not
always work out like this, however, for I also began to discover the
Turkish determination to give a solitary, outlandish-appearing walker
a lift: kindness in the heat; traditional hospitality; curiosity?

I was to travel on many a *dolmus* before I finished and they usually
proved to be an experience if not always fun. Ideally these little buses
were designed to seat twelve: two in the front bench seat beside the
driver, three and three in the next two rows and four across the
back. Most enterprising drivers, however, expected to cater for greater
numbers. Two small wooden boxes or stools would be used to complete
the two rows of three seats. After that, depending upon demand and
the degree of determination shown by the driver to obtain as many
fares as possible, extras would be cramed in, sometimes sorely trying
the patience of his original passengers. I travelled more than once with
someone half sitting on my knees, so cramped that I regretted taking
the lift at all. When a *dolmus* became full its driver would take it upon

himself to rearrange the seating so that still more passengers could be taken on board. It was generally considered to be a mark of favour if he invited a passenger to sit in the front; in fact, that was a place to be avoided since all too often, at least when I was in front, a friend of the driver would insist upon his perogative and squash into the limited space when two passengers were there already. The best seat was immediately behind the driver, against the window.

When I did take passage in a *dolmus* I would invariably be interrogated as to my nationality, age, journey, purpose and much else besides, depending upon the fluency or otherwise of the interpreter. More often than not this would be in German, by far the most common second language in the country. On such occasions I was normally offered cigarettes which I accepted and smoked; this allowed me to return the offer later on our journey: a *Samsun* or *Maltepe*. As long as they lasted I kept my English cigarettes in reserve for more special occasions.

My first stop after Vezirkopru was the small town of Duragan. Much work had been done on the road between the two towns; it was newly cut high up the steep valley-side above the river, for the waters of the Kizil Irmak were still rising here as a result of the dam at Kolay, now some 50 kilometres (30 miles) downstream. Deserted villages, half submerged by the rising waters, or isolated islands of land surrounded by the growing lake were dramatic evidence of the effect which the huge dam was already having many miles from its site. Shortly before the road reaches Duragan the Kizil Irmak takes a sharp V-turn to flow south-west. But there was no road alongside that stretch of river and I decided to go from Duragan to Boyabat and then double back down the other arm of the V to Khargi.

The landlord of the small hotel where I stayed in Duragan sat on my bed and begged for English cigarettes, so I gave him a few and then he treated me to tea. While exploring the back of the town up a hill I entered a small shop to purchase some grapes; the proprietor promptly asked me to sit and talk. He sent a boy to wash my grapes so that I could eat them on the spot. I offered him a cigarette; a friend joined us and we talked, although slowly for neither of them had any German and the friend had only a very inadequate smattering of English.

Later, back in the main square, I sat drinking lemon teas at a roadside table and was irritated by three small boys who gathered round to make fun of the foreigner. Public privacy is not easy to obtain, though even alone I sometimes found it almost impossible to write notes, read or examine my map without at once attracting onlookers who, moreover, were determined to be participants. They picked up my notes, pored over my map with me or seized my Turkish phrase-book to try their skill at English pronunciation. Each person in the group round me would insist on reading from it and they would appeal to me to judge who pronounced the English phrases the best. The result was that I could rarely learn any Turkish from it myself.

At first sight Duragan appeared to be a lazy place. Most members of the male population were in the tea-house sitting, talking, playing games and drinking tea. Few women were in evidence and those I saw were bustling about their work. After a while I escaped from the inquisitive trio of boys and found a less public tea-house where I was left to myself. On occasion, and Duragan was one such, I found that Turkish interest in strangers, the constant hospitality laced with its concomitant inquisitiveness, could be so overwhelming as to stifle. I just wanted to be left on my own.

Duragan seemed a curiously ingrown place. I noted a number of cripples: there was an oddly dark-faced blind man in the *lokanta* where I ate, a man with leprous skin and a tiny head, a misshapen dwarf who was a shoe black. In the evening when I returned to the tea-house where earlier I had been annoyed by the boys I was joined at my table by a madman who spent his time in flurries of action: tapping furiously with his feet or scratching his head in a curious circular motion only to stop suddenly and stare into space. There were endless numbers of boys in evidence but few women or girls. Atatürk did his best to emancipate women but old habits of female seclusion and male chauvinism die hard and the process still has a long way to go. In Duragan, as elsewhere, a woman or teenage girl dressed in western-style clothing was still very much the exception. On the streets and in public places Turkey remains a largely male society.

For a visitor such a small town may be picturesque and strange but for most of the inhabitants the boredom must often be extreme. So men sit chatting endlessly; one small glass of tea buys a place in the tea-house more or less indefinitely. And the fact that so many men are to be seen at all hours of the day relaxing in public places indicates the high level of unemployment which exists.

As I got used to the constant approaches by strangers who wished to question me, so I worked out techniques to deal with them. Some of my interrogators were far more interesting than others who merely wished to satisfy their curiosity while having little to tell me in return. Such exchanges also depended upon our language: who in the group could speak some German, English or French. When I got interested I would bring out my Turkish phrase-book or dictionary and then a conversation could be prolonged. But if it did not promise much I would answer the obvious first question and then, after a decent pause, excuse myself – turning back to my notes or map – in the hope that they would leave me in peace. This tactic worked quite well sometimes but its success or failure would depend upon whether a newcomer arrived to join the group and demanded to know about me. Then the interrogation would begin all over again.

From Duragan to Boyabat, from Boyabat to Khargi, from Khagi to Osmancik, similar experiences: getting into my walking stride; enjoying the camaraderie of travelling by crowded *dolmus* endless tea-house talks; looking for a technique to get rid of the boys who followed me through the town chanting 'What is your name?'. On the road to Khargi, when at last the river had dropped to its normal level, for it was too far upstream any longer to be affected by the rising waters of the dam I could see for the first time why it is called the Red River. It had become fast-running, bubbling, a rush of turbulent waters, red-brown with the silt it carried from somewhere far in the interior. Much of this road was also new, cut into the steep hillside 60–90 metres (200–300 feet) above the river. The waters at the dam had only reached two thirds of the way up the great barrage wall, so that this stretch of river was also destined to be affected at a later date when the lake had achieved its full size and depth.

I was shown round Osmancik by a German-speaking youth whose father had worked in Germany for 11 years; he was at school there and had come home for his summer holidays with the rest of the family. We had lunch together, then he took me round the town. A great rock dominates the centre of Osmancik and the castellated remains of an Ottoman fortress adorn its steep sides, while a huge silhouette of Atatürk that can be picked out by lights at night crowns the top of it. There was nothing particularly special about Osmancik but my guide was proud of it: he showed me the schools, the town-hall, the park. This was on another hill and we went to the top so that I could take photographs. Then we inspected a tiny mosque. Back in the centre of town we entered the main mosque, which was fairly modern and not especially interesting or attractive.

I hate mosquitoes and for me one of the abiding miseries of travel comes with that awful high-pitched whine which heralds their attacks. That night in Osmancik I was bitten to death, and since the hotel was also one of the dirtiest I have ever used I was up at the first light of dawn. For a while I sat on a little balcony which over-looked the main street; then I went for a walk. There is a fine stone bridge across the river at Osmancik and I crossed this in the still grey morning light to wander in some small streets on the other side. An officious, uniformed little man of Chaplin-like appearance asked me where I was going and pointed out that I was heading for a dead end; I shrugged and continued on my way. He went into a shop to purchase a loaf of bread, then came after me, offering me some – fresh baked bread was one of the constant pleasures of Turkey – and fell in beside me. Like everyone else he was simply curious. I did a circle and back at the bridge was hailed by a man sitting outside a tea-house so I joined him for the glass he offered me in exchange for some gentle probing.

From Osmancik I decided to go to Çorum. The town is away from the Kizil Irmak towards the centre of the area enclosed by the two rivers which constituted my boundaries. I felt that it was time for me to go 'inland' for a while, away from the line of the river, and from Çorum I intended to continue to Hattusas, the Hittite capital, so I took one of the long-distance buses from Osmancik to Çorum.

It is very easy to give offence, and I did so unwittingly that morning. I had breakfast in a small café next to my hotel and got into conversation with a young man who spoke quite good English. He told me there was a bus at nine o'clock to Çorum. When I had paid my bill and went to leave with my pack on my back – the bus station was only 200 yards away – he appeared beside me on a small Honda and offered to give me a lift to the bus. I estimated that it would be easier to walk with my pack and shoulder-bag than to balance them while I sat on the back of his Honda but when I said so, without a word he turned his machine and rode away. I had certainly not meant to rebuff his kindness.

The road to Çorum began along the river valley but then departed from it to wind up one of the spectacular mountain passes which make travel in Turkey so exciting. Over the pass the descent was slightly more gradual, the country open and bleak, rather like parts of the Scottish Highlands. Çorum lies in the centre of a plain. It turned out to be a big, bustling place. The author of one guidebook, in the astonishingly dismissive fashion adopted by those who instruct tourists about what they should or should not bother to see, devotes a line to Çorum, which he says is 'a large industrial town of no interest to the traveller'. I enjoyed it.

I stayed for three days in Çorum. I found an old but grand-looking hotel, the Mersin, in the centre of town and particularly asked for a room with a bath. They had one available – there was one such on each floor – and my bathroom was triangular in shape, a result of the building's odd architecture. The bath was of an ancient pattern and huge, the water beautifully hot. I washed all my clothes and had a long shower, a luxury I had not been able to obtain during the previous week at the small places in which I had stayed. I purchased some postcards and sent them off to people in England, visited the museum and looked at its Hittite artefacts. I bought grapes in the market from a surly Turk, for me a rarity to encounter. I explored generally and located a pleasant bar which I frequented when I wanted a beer, and changed some more travellers' cheques at the bank. I discovered that cake shops served breakfast – bread, honey, olives, cheese – as opposed to the usual soup on offer in *lokantas*. On a long walk through the outer part of the town early on the Sunday morning I came upon two old men playing a pipe and a drum. They had an appreciative audience of small children and while I paused to watch I had a shouted conversation with two youths on a balcony above me. They wanted all the usual information, or my potted life story, and for a change I told them things which were quite untrue. I watched a chain of men and boys throwing huge green water-melons from a piled truck to an open store on a square, where the owner piled them with artistic exactitude.

Then I came upon a lively cattle market and took a number of pictures, including several of men who simply wanted to be in my photographs: they did not ask for copies to be sent to them from England. I came upon a drunken beggar who happily posed for me to photograph, but only after I had provided him with the means for further drinking. A maze of small old streets meandered uphill behind my hotel and I wandered through them for hours: the upper storeys overhung the streets, tiny mosques nestled among the houses, women in two-thirds purdah looked at my camera shyly, wondering what to do if I pointed it at them, and, occupying an entire side of one small square of brightly-painted houses, gleamed banked rows of white sheepskins out to dry.

Back on the main street I watched donkey carts pass with drums banging as a smiling wedding party went by: they all turned as one when I raised my camera. Over a meal I found myself thinking of the many things (writing and lecturing) I would have to do on my return to England and then I laughed. On this trip I had decided that planning – both immediate and long-term – was out. So instead I watched the animated Çorum scene, enjoying as extraordinary what for the Turks was everyday. That is the great pleasure of travel.

# 10

# Sungurlu: Hattusas and the Hittites

The main road from Çorum to Sungurlu was interesting but not spec-tacular and I made the journey by bus. I chose Sungurlu as the nearest town of any size to Hattusas; I was still far 'inland' from the Kizil Irmak. Sungurlu lies to the side of the main Çorum to Ankara road and when I got off the bus a French-speaking man approached, ready with a taxi to take me to Hattusas. 'At least,' and he indicated a dark-haired young man, 'my driver will take you'. I excused myself and walked into the town. But he would be waiting, he repeated, willing to take me at any time. Hattusas was some 40 kilometres distant.

I walked up a hill into the busy market-town and a young school girl – a change from the endless boys – fell in beside me. She had good English and chatted away until we reached the centre of the town. There was an undistinguished-looking hotel which would, I knew, be far cheaper than the 'tourist' motel on the outskirts of town which the bus had passed. It was cheap: its interior was also coated in a layer of dust like a carpet. The receptionist was a teenage boy who claimed to speak French; he got stuck at once. After I had settled in I went to the more pretentious motel for lunch, where I sat on a balcony overlooking a swimming pool where Turkish tourists were enjoying themselves. As far as I could judge there were no foreigners about except for myself. The chef came to speak German with me. The meal was indifferent but the beer was good.

Sungurlu was crowded and busy. I wandered through its two main streets, exchanged greetings with three curious policemen, and was then approached in the main square by a young man who asked: 'Was I French? German? English?' He knew what I was perfectly well.

'English', I said.

'Would I mind talking with him? He was a student and wished to practise his languages.'

'Not in the least,' I said. 'What should we discuss?' This set him back.

'It is good to talk English, I do not get the opportunity,' he said.

'You speak it well', I replied, and waited.

'Are you here on a visit?'

'Yes, I am.'

'Are you going – ', then he paused; it was too soon. 'Do you like Turkey?' he substituted, lamely.

'Yes, I do indeed,' Again I waited. My tactics were not helping him and he was becoming increasingly stilted.

Another dark-haired young man was sitting casually nearby – we were on a low wall at the side of the square – and my student now turned to him: 'This is my friend, he says you want to go out to Hattusas.' I looked at the dark-haired young man: 'Of course, the taxi driver!' We shook hands.

'How much will your friend charge?' I asked.

'He is very reasonable; twenty thousand lira.'

'Perhaps I can find someone who will take me out for less,' I said.

'No one is cheaper than my friend. His uncle who is the next cheapest charges twenty-five thousand lira.' There was a pause while I stared thoughtfully into the middle distance. 'If you take my friend's taxi I would come with you: I know Hattusas very well, I used to act as a guide. I would do so for you – not for money – but to practise my English.'

'You mean the taxi will take me there and back, and you will come and act as a guide, all for twenty thousand lira?'

'Yes', he nodded. They waited.

'All right', and I agreed. They sighed audibly with relief. It had been a well-worked-out, determined approach: there were not many tourists about, and it suited both them and me.

So they drove me to the fabled Hattusas, the fortress hilltop capital of the Hittities from which, more than 3,500 years ago, these little-known people spread their empire as far as the Gulf and the Syrian coast of the Mediterranean. For most people, even today when so much more is known, the Hittites make only a fleeting historical appearance in the Old Testament as yet another of the enemies of the Israelites, either smiting or being smitten. In fact, they enjoyed two major periods of power spanning some 600 years altogether. The Old Kingdom was at its zenith from 1750 to 1500 BC; the New Kingdom from 1350 to 1200. Agriculture and shepherding were the chief occu-pations of the Hittites as they are of the Turks in central Anatolia today. Fighting might be added to the list. Their code of laws shows a genuine humaneness in the prescribed punishments and the Hittites are credited with the first known impartial historical narratives. It was about 1600 BC that Murshilish moved the Hittite capital from Kushshar to Hattusas. At the battle of Kadesh on the Orontes (1298 BC) the Hittites and the Egyptians fought each other to a stalemate though both claimed the victory. The two empires reluctantly recognised parity, and it was then that the Hittities reached the summit of their power.

They were an extraordinary people. About 1531 BC a Hittite army marched its way 800 kilometres (500 miles) down the Euphrates to destroy Babylon. Then it went home again. It was not conquest but a demonstration of military might to overawe neighbours. Later they were pushed back to their heartland contained within the circle of the Halys river. Then, from 1380 BC onwards, under Suppiluliumus I, they staged a revival.

For centuries the Hittites enjoyed a virtual monopoly of iron which they forged from the ore mined along the northern shores of Asia Minor, east of the Halys. Iron weapons, plus their heavy war chariots, gave them military superiority for several centuries. They disappeared from history before the Sea Peoples whose great migrations about 1200 BC changed the face of the ancient world. The Etruscans who arrived in Italy about 900 BC are believed to be descendants of the Hittites.

Bleak and forbidding, the site of Hattusas is awesome. The fortress city, with its massive 1.6 kilometre (1 mile)-long walls, was set on a great hill which dominates a cup-like basin rimmed with further hills. The view stretches for miles. At 1,060 metres (3,500 feet) the setting for this massive citadel is bleak at the best of times; in winter when the Anatolian snows cover the region it is a place to leave. One of the wonders of history is what makes some people expand with such aggressive thoroughness. The setting of Hattusas supplies at least part of the answer. That extensive capital with its lion and sphinx gates and enormous temple site with a channel cut in stone for the sacrificed bulls' blood to drain away could have existed only as the centre of an empire which paid for such isolated magnificence.

My taxi-driver and student guide did me proud. They whisked me from site to site; we chatted with their friends at the entrance, who gave me water-melon to eat; they warned me against touts with newly-discovered Hittite coins; they talked too much. As we were leaving the ruins of the temple a couple passed us and the woman, who was wearing a large old-fashioned floppy hat said 'Hello'.

Surprised, I turned to my student guide and asked: 'Do you know that English woman?'

'No,' he was startled, 'she was talking to you.' I had ignored her. Now I realised that she was the English lady with whom I had exchanged nods on the deck of the *Truva*. I had not meant to be rude; I had simply not recognised her. I wonder what she thought.

# 11

# Back to the Kizil Irmak: the Buluts of Haçilar

Fifty-one kilometres (31 miles) from Sungurlu, lying on the banks of the river, is the village of Kizilirmak, and I headed for this the next day. On my return from Hattusas I had purchased bread, tomatoes and fruit; I was up at five-thirty in the morning. I had a snack, packed, and left the hotel at a quarter to six. The receptionist and various assorted friends of his were sprawled in sleep on the huge dirty chairs of the reception area but I had paid my bill the night before. I cannot recall any place to compare with that hotel for concentrated dust.

I had quite a long walk to clear the town. There were plenty of early workers about, mainly farmers, and the tea-houses were busy. I was tempted to stop for tea, but decided to press on as I had a long walk ahead of me. After 6 or 7 kilometres (3 or 4 miles) I took a rest by one of the roadside drinking taps which are set in concrete, by small streams. Then I began to rise into bleak, treeless hills. It was wheat country, a rolling prairie of endless waving wheat, except where it had been harvested: then the close-cropped fields looked like soldiers' heads.

I now began to encounter a steady stream of tractors coming into Sungurlu. Most of them pulled trailers and these had a complement of passengers, sometimes a full load. The drivers stared their astonishment at me as I walked past them with my pack on my back and many made a sign with their raised hands, a sign with which I was to become extremely familiar. It meant a number of things: query, astonishment, disbelief. I waved or nodded and walked on.

Soon a tractor came in my direction and the driver stopped to offer me a lift. I mounted the trailer and we travelled perhaps 2 kilometres (1 mile) before he had to turn off into his fields. He told me that I should wait at the roadside for a lift and not walk as I had been doing when he came along. He had no German and our conversation was difficult but very clearly he was saying: 'Do not walk; there is no need.' He pointed to where I should take up my station while I waited for the next lift. I did not attempt to explain that I liked walking; this, I think, was a consideration which never occurred to the many Turks who insisted upon giving me lifts. I waited at the roadside until he had driven his tractor out of sight and then, once more, began walking up the hill.

The road took dramatic twists through the ridge of hills until it reached the village of Karacay, 17 kilometres (10 miles) from Sungurlu. Then I had to walk a further 7 or 8 kilometres (4 or 5 miles) before descending into a broad flat valley. A great truck now drew up alongside me and the driver signalled for me to mount. The second half of the road to the river was accomplished in 15 minutes. I took a photograph of the driver standing at the front of his truck; then he was off with a cheery wave. He was going to Çankiri. I entered a distinctly dirty, fly-blown tea-house. Conversation stopped dead and I was treated to careful inspection by the whole room. There was nowhere to sit for every table was full but a boy produced a chair and two men invited me to join them at their table. I did so, shook hands and began a slow, careful conversation in answer to their questions. Tea was brought and gradually the other occupants of the room returned to their talk or games: cards and the game of *Okey* were in progress at two thirds of the tables. *Okey* was very popular and I saw it played in many of the tea-houses. It requires four players and each man has a wooden rack upon which he arranges his pieces in two rows. These are like large dominoes with white faces, upon which numbers are carved; different colours are used for each number. The players enjoy slapping their pieces loudly upon the table. When I went to pay the proprietor waved my offer aside but I was not sure, either then or on later, similar occasions, whether the tea was on the house or whether one of the men in the room had signalled that he would pay for me, something that was to happen many times. Turkish generosity could be embarrassing and sometimes I had to choose between asking for another drink, when I knew someone else would insist upon paying, or going thirsty.

As I reached the outskirts of the sprawling village a tractor and trailer came along; the driver stopped at the command of one of his passengers, a man who spoke German, and insisted that I took a lift with them. We continued for about a kilometre (half a mile) until the tractor turned away from the river, when I got out to walk again. The dirt road now ran parallel to the river, which was about 1.6 kilometres

(1 mile) distant. I had covered no more than 2 or 3 kilometres (1 or 2 miles) when a *dolmus*, tight-packed with passengers, drew to a stop beside me. 'Where was I going?' I began to explain 'nowhere in particular, just along the river', but that was too puzzling so they found space in the front seat and once more I was being given a lift. We went perhaps 4 kilometres (2 miles) to a village and then I was invited to get out by a superior, German-speaking man who had orchestrated the questions which the others had put to me. The *dolmus* departed with most of its complement of passengers while I accompanied the German speaker to his home. He was back on a holiday from Germany, where he had been working for 15 years.

His was a small, ordinary village house but it was liberally supplied with an assortment of stereo and other electronic goods, the fruits of his labours in a foreign land. He had no idea when he would come back to Turkey again, he told me, and he needed all the money he earned for his family. I imagined that the claims those back at home made upon him – and others of the more successful Turks who are Gastarbeiter in Germany – are both considerable and pressing.

He produced *ayran*, a drink which I found more and more refreshing the longer I travelled in the country. I had three glasses, admired his various electronic goods and then bid him goodbye and set forth once more. Like a number of those I met who had been in Germany he was anxious to demonstrate his prosperity to me. The fact that he could also talk with me in German added to his prestige in the village, and for both reasons he had wanted to make me his guest.

Again I walked and again after about 3 kilometres (2 miles) I was given a lift. Another tractor pulling a trailer tightly crowded with about 20 farm workers had passed me and then, at the insistence of a tough-looking elderly man of perhaps 60, had come to a jolting halt. So I scrambled aboard. My 'host' had a seamed, nut-brown face, close-cropped white hair, and deep bright eyes: if not piercing they were certainly busy searching me for information but in that rattling noisy trailer – he had no German – conversation was not really possible. After 2 kilometres (1 mile) we stopped at the village of Haçilar and my new friend said '*ekmek*' (food) and invited me to follow him. He heaved a large heavy sack across his shoulders and we set off down a path which led at right angles from the road towards the centre of the village.

We had only gone a short distance when a very pretty teenage girl came to greet the man; we stopped and she took the sack from him and herself heaved it along before her. We turned into a farmyard whose house had a fine first-floor balcony. My host invited me up and at the top of the steps I removed my boots. Then I sat on the wide bench that ran along one side of the balcony, which was square, the shape and size of a substantial room. It provided a splendid view to a range of bleak, blue hills perhaps 16 kilometres (10 miles) distant across the valley.

Family now appeared: small boys in fair numbers, very pretty teenage girls, older women. Here the women came forward to shake hands with me, something other women had avoided on earlier occasions. A large jug of *ayran* was produced for us to drink and then with seemingly miraculous speed a magnificent meal was laid before us: tomato omelette, green peppers, goat's cheese, bread and tea. My host was a Bulut. By the time we had come to the end of our meal word had spread and friends and relatives began to arrive for a visit – and to inspect me. One of these latter arrivals was a vivacious young woman who spoke quite good English and taught in a primary school in Çankiri. Gulcihan was her name and she acted as chief interpreter.

A tall, elegant man with a small grey moustache, friendly quizzical eyes and an easy smile now joined us. He was a brother to Saban Bulut, my host. More tea was produced; then I took a photograph of the whole family, Saban sitting upright and proud in the centre of the group. The day had become very hot and he suggested a rest – even with my various lifts I had walked between 25 and 30 kilometres (15 and 18 miles). Before resting, however, he had given me a gift. I had taken my boots off when I arrived and was just wearing thick walking socks, but as it happened they were my oldest pair and had more than one hole in them. Saban went into the house and reappeared with a pair of magnificent thick white wool socks: he indicated the less than elegant appearance of those I wore and everybody laughed as I accepted his gift. Now he showed me into the family's best room, where I lay down on a spotless divan. There was a large television set on a table against one wall: it had been covered with a cloth as though waiting to have a meal set upon it. I must have slept almost at once.

I awoke about an hour later. There were quite a few people on the veranda when I went out and each of the newcomers shook hands with me. Gulcihan took charge as they began to question me. 'Why was I in Turkey?' they wanted to know, and while trying to answer this question I remembered the letter which Muhurrem Koc, the foreman at the dam, had written for me. I produced this and passed it round.

Gulcihan was scornful: 'Who wrote this?' she demanded. She would have given poor Koc a rough time in her class for his indifferent grammar. So the letter was dismissed and returned to me. But it had served its end and helped explain my purpose.

Saban invited me to stay for the night – by then it was late afternoon. More people came while others departed, so that there was constant coming and going on the large veranda. The brother whose name I never learnt (or perhaps in all the introductions I had missed it) now joined me again and a meal was provided just for the two of us. I dubbed him 'Uncle'; he had a little English and liked to look up words in my small dictionary. The two of us would be laboriously conversing – English, Turkish, dictionary – when Gulcihan would interrupt impatiently to take charge. She rapidly became excited and then she would snatch the dictionary from one of our hands and show her familiarity with such a book by the speed with which she found the appropriate word. When I was talking with someone else and she wished to bring my attention back to the dictionary and the conversation which she was conducting on behalf of everyone else she would cry: '*Mr Guy, Mr Guy*', until I turned to her again.

'Uncle' now excused himself: he had to attend to the family grave, he said, for there was a religious festival the next day and everyone would be celebrating. This, I think, explained why so many members of the family were about in their best clothes and not out working on the farm. He left, and two young men, Bulut cousins I discovered, now took charge of me. 'Would I like to go and visit their fields?' I assented with alacrity for by then I had been answering questions for more than an hour and was exhausted by the process. So they unhitched a tractor from a trailer in the corner of the farmyard and the three of us set off, one young Bulut driving, his cousin and I sitting on the two mudguards of the huge wheels.'

The soils of that wide river valley were rich and here water-melons predominated. We drove 2 or 3 kilometres (1 or 2 miles) back along the road I had travelled earlier in the day and then up on to the sloping hillside. We walked over a huge field of water-melons ready for harvesting and selected a large ripe specimen which the three of us cut into slices and consumed. Across the valley the setting sun was painting a kaleidoscope of colours on the distant hills. We had another water-melon. The two young men were pleased to be away from the elders of the family and were content to show me things and eat water-melons without subjecting me to the endless questioning which their teacher cousin Gulcihan insisted upon conducting. When we had finished eating we roared off on the tractor – I found that most Turks drove their tractors at maximum speed, at least when they were using them, as now, for general travel purposes rather than in the fields – and crossed the road to take another path down to the Kizil Irmak. The river was high and swift-flowing. One of the young men stripped off and went for a swim, but he kept to a side pool where the strong current would not carry him downstream.

Back at the farm, 'Uncle' came to take me to his house for the evening. We walked through the village and before entering his house sat against a dried mud wall at a regular village meeting place. Various men from the village would drift up, shake hands and join us for a while. A boy with some German was produced to act as interpreter. The mosquitoes and sand-flies became worse and worse so that we spent half our time vainly slapping after we had been bitten. An extraordinary two-storey house leaned crazily nearby. A stork's nest occupied a corner of the roof and the two storks on it doubled their long necks backwards and then clicked their beaks endlessly in the chattering sign they make to each other. Answering clicks came from other stork nests in the village.

When visiting, as at the present time, I would always carry my shoulder-bag with me since it contained three vital aids to social inter-course: my camera. the map and the dictionary. Each had a function to play on such occasions, and now in the fading light I took out my camera. Not knowing the ownership of the crazy house I said I wanted a picture of the storks but 'Uncle' smiled and said: 'I think it is the house you want.'

We now played a word game. Someone in the group would point at an object and give its Turkish name and I would then supply the English equivalent. The game was made enjoyable by our mutual inability to pronounce each others' languages with any degree of accuracy. As we were doing this a flock of gobbling turkeys wandered round the corner of the leaning house I had just photographed. Some-one laughed, pointed at them and gave the Turkish name. They turned to me. I knew I was in trouble, but there was no escape and I said 'turkey'. They looked puzzled, thinking I had misunderstood, and for a second time a man pointed at the ungainly birds. I shrugged and prefaced my remark by saying I did not understand how it had come about but – '*turkey*'. I had no explanation for the use of the word turkey to describe the bird although I thought it was that originally the birds had been brought to England from Turkey and I said so. There was an awkward silence and then 'Uncle' changed the subject.

Finally we all went in the dark to his house and sat in a large long room with a television at one end, so that we were like a small cinema audience, but though the screen was active, for most of the time we talked and ignored it. I suppose the need to have it on was social: some of those present watched. Gulcihan asked the most questions. 'Uncle', in his own quiet way, dominated the gathering. The food was excellent and varied. At last, well after midnight, when I had promised Gulcihan and others to send photographs, 'Uncle' lit my path by torch back through the village to Saban's house. There I was given the divan in the front room.

# 12

# A Holiday in Sarimbey

I had told my host that I wished to be off early to take advantage of the cool of the day and I was up at six o'clock. One of the women brought me hot milk to drink; then I said goodbye to Saban, who had risen specially for my departure. It was a holiday and they had invited me to spend it with them but I did not wish to overstay my welcome. 'Uncle' walked with me through the village to set me on my road – this was a courtesy but it was often necessary as well, for as I had discovered more than once it was easy to become lost in the turnings of even a small village.

I normally found the first hour of walking to be the most enjoyable of the day. It was still cool and some of the hillsides had not yet emerged from the shadows while the rays of the rising sun would suddenly catch a distant object – a bend of the river or a village nestling under a hill – to bring it to sparkling life and alter the pattern unfolding before me.

The next village on my road was 7 kilometres (4 miles) distant and by the time I approached it the increasing heat of the sun made me look in my shoulder-bag for my hat; I discovered that I had left it behind at the Bulut house, but by then I had come too far to go back. I would feel its loss. I did not wish to pause for I had got nicely into my kilometre-eating stride and in any case the road left the village off to one side. I hoped to get through without a break as the urge to make distance was upon me, but this was not to be. I was hailed from a hundred metres away and a young man hurried up to insist that I returned with him for some refreshment. I protested that I had only just begun my day's walk but to no avail: in any case, why not? I went back with him through an impressive, fortress-like wooden gateway into a farmyard and then up on to a balcony. Chairs were arranged. As I took off my pack I wondered how long this stop would last. My host sprinkled eau-de-cologne on my hands, then a tray of sweets was produced, to be followed by a samovar of tea. 'Are you hungry?', he asked, but I assured him that I was not.

The young man's mother now appeared, a neighbour spotted us on the balcony and came in to say hello, and then an old man, who must have been in his eighties, came to sit beside me. He had on an ill-fitting best suit, while pinned to his breast was a red triangle of ribbon supporting a medal. He was dressed for a holiday occasion. Slowly, for conversation with him was not easy, I learnt that the medal which he displayed proudly for me was the independence award given to those who had fought to bring Atatürk to power in 1923.

On the other side of the high wooden wall surrounding the yard below me several men were busy skinning two large sheep which they had just killed. These were hanging by their rear legs while their skins were stripped expertly from their bodies with a minimum of wasted motion. Here, too, everyone was preparing for the festival.

I had one eye on the sheep-skinning while I gave the rest of my attention to the old man as together we laboriously reconstructed the great days of Atatürk's revolution. We were in the middle of this exercise when a *dolmus* drove into the dirt road beside the big gate and to my surprise 'Uncle' appeared; he waved and came up on to the balcony. He had brought my hat. He was greeted and given tea; then he told me how he had thought to find me about 2 or 3 kilometres (1 or 2 miles) beyond the village, but after they had continued for at least 5 he realised I must be here, so they had returned. Everyone knew where I was. 'Uncle' then insisted that his driver friend would give me a lift beyond the next village 'because of its dogs'. I took leave of my host and the old man and set off again, in this case receiving a lift especially designed for my benefit.

We passed through the next village where fierce dogs raced alongside the *dolmus* as it wound slowly through the narrow streets; some of them wore huge iron collars with long spikes sticking out of them. The thought occurred to me that they might have been less than friendly had I walked through the village on foot. Then, perhaps 15 kilometres (9 miles) from the village where I had just been entertained, we came to Sarimbey. 'Uncle' had been a little disingenuous: his real motive for the long lift was not just to ensure that I passed safely through the village of dogs but to deposit me with some relatives, I think cousins, in Sarimbey. We drove into an astonishing farmyard, where balconies faced each other across the yard at different levels; the higher balcony was built in front of a large granary. These two sides were double-storeyed and connected on the third side by a low lying wing of the rambling house in which the kitchens were situated. It was possible to walk on the kitchen roof and then on to the second, higher balcony. Everywhere, or so it seemed, steep wooden steps led up or down to a bewildering number of levels. The whole must have been a child's paradise, providing endless corners in which to hide.

An extensive, or extended, family was in the process of gathering for the festival. This, I discovered, though not without considerable difficulty, was the Festival of the Sacrifice (Abraham and Isaac) when public holidays for three (or four) days closed everything down. After introductions 'Uncle' had tea, then said goodbye and departed. In a corner of the yard below a sheep was being skinned. My host, Mustafa, was a teacher at a big secondary school in Kirrikale. He had a brother or cousin of roughly the same age who was also a teacher. Every generation was present that day, ages ranging from very young children, a number of teenagers, several young men and women in their twenties, to older men and women in their fifties and sixties and finally the patriarch of the family, the great-grandfather whom I discovered to be ninety.

A first, simple meal was produced at about ten thirty. This was a running feast – stewed mutton and rice – for people were arriving all the time. Gradually a group settled themselves on the veranda round me and began the serious task of questioning me. I had no idea what 'Uncle' had told them. When they got excited – the teachers had some English and my dictionary was out, being passed rapidly from hand to hand – they would all start asking questions at once. I would try to answer one question while two more were thrown at me, so I would pass from question one to question three and then the person responsible for question two would insist upon an answer. They enjoyed it and so did I in a way but it was extremely hard work and I was the one who had to do the work. I had reached the point where I could understand the thrust of a Turkish question even if I knew few of the words. Occasionally, when I did produce the correct Turkish word or phrase, I earned generous applause.

Storks on a nearby roof-top had begun clicking their beaks as though sending endless morse code messages and I thought to take a photograph. The sight of my camera brought the particular conversation of the moment to an abrupt end: would I take a photograph . . . or two . . . or three? I would. I suggested a family group on the lower balcony – the sun was just about in the right place by then if they moved well to the front by the rail – and I went across to the other balcony. The old man was carefully settled in the centre, sitting upright, stern, patriarchal and proud while the rest of the large family, or at least those who were then present, grouped round him.

As soon as the photography session had come to an end more food was served. This was the real feast. Most of the older women had been busy in the dark kitchen and the girls now brought an array of dishes up on to the balcony where the men all sat round in high expectation: shish kebab, rice, unleavened and fresh bread, spring onions, salad, and stewed mutton as well as plates of various delicacies whose exact provenance I found difficult to determine. I was ceremoniously handed one especially revolting-looking morsel – not an eye – which in fact tasted delicious. While we were all busy eating the relentless questioning fell off, and for this I was grateful. Eventually the meat dishes were cleared away and slices of fresh melon were served. Finally the samovar of tea was brought out and the smokers lit up.

By the time the feast was over the sun had shifted to glare fiercely upon us beneath the eaves of the balcony so we moved across the yard to the second balcony, which was in the shade. Conversation became more desultory as everyone began to nod. The call of the village muezzin came loud and near – there was a little mosque not far from the farm. As it happened I was sitting cross-legged at the time and my school-teacher friend gently tapped my knee and indicated that I should uncross my legs. Later when the muezzin had ceased he told me that it was all right to cross them again!

In answer to my query two teenage boys said they would take me to the Kizil Irmak, which I thought was behind the line of trees which we could see winding along the broad expanse of the valley about a kilometre (half a mile) below the village. In fact this was only a tributary and the river was 5 kilometres (3 miles) further off across the wide valley. The three of us meandered through fields by the small stream and past an old broken-down mill while the boys named the fruits and vegetables that were growing there: apples, pears, grapes, water-melon, melon, beans, peas, horseradish, potatoes – it was a rich farming area and their own farm had a wide variety of crops. Then we walked back through the village and up on to the hill beyond where a white water-tower crowned the summit.

Back at the house everyone was sleeping or nodding. Mustafa insisted I should have a rest and I was shown into the best room where I slept on a divan for an hour and a half. When I reappeared I was at once served with another meal. Mustafa and one or two others joined me in this; then Mustafa said he would take me to see his fields. His father and daughter came as well. It was after six but the sun still shone brightly from a cloudless blue sky as it sank behind the hills. Everything stood out in sharp yet soft-coloured relief, and the temperature was dropping fast after the long hot day. We drove several kilometres up a spectacular path and then wandered through an enormous field of ripe sunflowers, their huge heavy heads drooping to pull the great stalks over and downwards. We collected several heads to take back so that we could eat the seeds.

In the house everyone was crowded into one room to watch the television. Another meal of mutton, salad and water-melon was served – it was a day of eating – followed by tea. The old man now came in and went to his corner. One of the teenage girls brought a large plastic bowl and filled it with hot water, and 'Bapa' removed his socks to rest his feet in it. More questions directed to me, this time about British politics and *Mrs Thatcher*; then the old man retired to bed and I said my goodbye to him, for he would not be about in the morning when I departed. Mustafa suggested that we went out on to the balcony again, so we sat there in darkness except for a bright moon which cast weird shadows across the yard. We opened sunflower seeds and ate the kernels.

Finally we all retired to bed: it was midnight and the next day was still another holiday so no one was in any hurry. I shared the best room with one of the cousins who had come for the feast from another village. This time I could not sleep; I thought instead of my hosts: generous, inquisitive, full of fun. They were also money-conscious; this was a rich farm and the younger members of the family were at high school obtaining good education. They were intrigued to make comparisons of money with Britain and would ask me to give equivalent British salaries for teachers or farmers. The difference between the figures I supplied and those for Turkey were so great that they gasped. Mustafa told me how little he received as a secondary school teacher. He had shown me over the extensive family farm with considerable pride.

As I had discovered on this particular stretch of the journey as well as previously, it was extremely difficult to walk on my own. The Turks simply would not believe that I wanted to walk and constantly offered – thrust upon me might be a better way to put it – lifts, whether I showed any desire for them or not. During the day I discovered just how difficult it was to be alone, even for a moment. If I rose to stretch my legs or wandered off to find the outside lavatory someone would come to assist me, in the French sense of the word. The endless questioning was tiring. By then I had overcome my initial resentment at the constant, prying questions and was ready for them, but I did find the process extremely wearing. To be questioned about your personal life, your impression of Turkey, British politics, the chances for Turkey entering the European Community, the Russians or the Americans all in quick succession from half a dozen people at once when the conversation had to be conducted in a mixture of English, German, Turkish and intelligent sign language with frequent reference to a tiny dictionary was hard work. By the end of such a day I was ready for a rest, and sometimes I would have preferred just to be left alone, but that was not to be.

# 13

# Ankara

Only with difficulty had I persuaded Mustafa that I should leave at six o'clock the next morning. I woke as usual with the first light, and quietly dressed and packed so as not to disturb the other guest who was sharing the room with me. I need not have worried for he slept soundly until I left. Mustafa sat talking with me while we waited for tea, which his mother had got up to make. When she appeared with the tea she expressed amazement, but whether at my early rising or the fact that I was determined to walk I do not know. There was no sign of the rest of the family; they were enjoying their holiday in sleep. Mustafa now walked to the edge of the village with me. A long straight road stretched away for several kilometres before rising to cross a gentle hill beyond which lay the next village.

There was little traffic about and I walked at a fast pace enjoying the silence of early day. Mustafa had told me that whatever I did I should not stop in the next village which, he said, was in quarantine. I tried in vain to discover for what but he merely repeated the word 'quarantine' as though the village suffered from the plague. When I did come to it two men sat smoking by the well, which also acted as the bus-stop. They hailed me and despite the quarantine I joined them for a smoke. They asked where I had stayed the night before, and the fact that I had been a guest in the farm at Sarimbey impressed them; I suspect that my hosts were important local people. While we were talking a *dolmus* came by and one of the men rushed out into the middle of the road to stop it. He called me over: 'This will take you to Sulakuyrt'; he turned to me triumphantly.

'But I want to walk.'

'Walk?' His voice became incredulous.

'Well, why not? It is only a few kilometres.'

He looked at me in astonishment: 'But the *dolmus* will take you.'

The driver, meanwhile, shrugged good naturedly and took out a ciga-rette. He would wait while we talked it out.

It was a typical situation: a friendly, over-zealous Turk busy organis-ing me. The trouble was I did not wish to be organised. Sometimes on such occasions those who insisted upon what I should do became quite angry if I refused. This time, in the end, I walked, and there were no hard feelings although the man who had stopped the *dolmus* did look dubiously at me, unsure just what to make of such oddness.

Sulakuyrt was a pretty little place but, though at first tempted to stay, I decided instead to press on to Kirrikale which was 50 kilometres (30 miles) distant. I found a local bus which was due to leave soon and took a seat in it. The bus filled quite rapidly, then, when each person had secured a seat, they drifted away again, disappearing into tea-houses or shops in the square until the driver gave a number of blasts on his hooter when everyone rushed back.

At last, it seemed, we were ready to go. The driver now took us perhaps 50 metres down a dead-end road and stopped. A big man got in, greeted the driver's mate as though they had not met in years, and launched into an animated conversation about their respective families. We backed for 20 metres and more people got in. We returned to the original starting point. There the big man said goodbye to his friend and got out. He was not coming. Finally we departed. The road was a pleasant one and we stopped frequently to pick up passengers until we came to the main Ankara-Yozgat road. Once we had turned on to that there was no more stopping until we reached Kirrikale, a substan-tial city with a population of 320,000.

I never really came to grips with Kirrikale, which earns only the briefest of mentions in guidebooks. It is modern, sprawling, untidy, a drab industrial town. I wandered round the centre until I had decided which hotel to stay in. This was clean and pleasant and my room had a balcony, so I took a bath, washed some clothes and then sat on the balcony to write notes. Later I went out to explore the town, only to find that almost everything was shut: we were still in the middle of the Festival of the Sacrifice. The day was exceptionally hot so I had an ice-cream as I walked the town. It was not good. I stopped at a small kiosk for a drink of Fanta, which was lukewarm. I found a small *lokanta* for lunch and that was a disappointment too.

Back in the hotel I sat on my balcony reading and watching the shop on the other side of the street, two storeys below; this was not closed for the holiday and had a constant stream of customers. It dealt in sheepskins. A man with a horse and cart stopped outside the shop. He was delivering several bloody sheepskins, the result of the ongoing festival, which had been thrown into the back of his open cart. The proprietor of the shop came out to finger the skins. The two men talked and arrived at a price, then the owner took the skins into the shop and collected his money. He drove off, although I could not tell from above whether he felt he had got a good bargain or not. The stench of the skins rose to my balcony but after a while it became indistinguishable from all the other smells. My eyes were hurting and I discovered that one had become very bloodshot, presumably the effect of dictionary conversations: the print was exceptionally small and the light in the houses in Sarimbey and earlier had been dim, not designed for reading, so that I had strained my eyes.

Later in the hotel lounge I talked with the young receptionist. He pored over my map and, once he knew roughly where I intended to go, insisted upon telling me the places where I had to stop for historic or scenic reasons. He told me that the Kizil Irmak had a bad reputation: it was a sad, dangerous river. There is a song about it: two young lovers who have just married are crossing a bridge over the river followed by all their wedding guests when the bridge collapses and everyone is drowned.

I wanted to visit Ankara, although it was off my river route. I had some business to do and in any case felt that the capital city justified a trip. I decided to travel by train. I had just asked a young man the way to the station when I was hailed by several of the men from Sarimbey; they were in town on business with tractor and trailer. We shook hands and they wished me a good journey. My informant was so impressed by this encounter that he insisted upon walking to the station with me. There, when he had checked the time of the train, he bought me a drink of Fanta and stayed to see me off.

The train, which I think came from Sivas, was crowded but I found a seat in a carriage otherwise occupied by a sleeping family. At first we followed the Kizil Irmak back downstream along its gorge, which is spectacular at this point. Then, after the town of Irmak, we headed west for Ankara. The journey of 30 kilometres (43 miles) took nearly three hours but a tea man plied his wares along the corridor and, once they had woken up, I got into conversation with the family in my compartment. For part of the journey the railway ran high along a hillside overlooking a deep valley.

Rarely did I set off on a journey in Turkey without enjoying spectacular scenery. My road might appear to pass through flat uninteresting countryside but never for long. A sudden twist and what had begun as a gentle rising hill became an escarpment, while the road was suddenly cutting through cliffs, twisting and turning at the head of a gorge or rising sheer through hairpin bends.

I spent two days in Ankara, which has none of the fascination of Istanbul. Most of it is modern, sprawling for miles over its hills. The only intriguing part is the citadel and I spent hours wandering its narrow steep streets. The old *Bedesten* with its restored domes is now the Museum of Anatolian Cultures and its collection displays every age of Asia Minor from the early Bronze Age through each new period of empire and conquest down to Ottoman times.

# 14

# Bala

After my interlude in Ankara I decided that I would rejoin my route of march at Bala rather than returning to the river at Kirrikale. I began the day badly by going to the wrong bus terminal, but eventually found the correct bus – it was hot and with my pack I was soon perspiring freely. Bala is about 65 kilometres (40 miles) from Ankara and, as I discovered, situated on a high ridge. I travelled on one of the large long-distance buses, the kings of the road in Turkey. The first part of the ride was dusty and boring, along a great highway out of the capital, but later we turned into a smaller and more spectacular route to rise steadily until reaching Bala, which is 1,300m (4,265 feet) above sea-level.

Bala was in sight for some considerable distance before we reached it: the town is spread out along a hilltop and is dominated at one end by a huge grain silo, which stood silhouetted against the clear, brilliant sky. It is strange how often you can look at something without realising what it is. I have seen many grain silos, yet as even our giant bus was forced to toil slowly up the steep hills that led to Bala I was puzzled about the huge square keep-like structure, and only as we came into the main street did I realise what it was.

I found Bala a strange town. The bus deposited me in the centre of the main street and was off at once – I was the only person to descend – and I found the street lined from end to end with a huge queue of tractors and trailers, each of the latter filled level with grain. They were in a long line waiting their turn to be weighed and emptied into the silo. Bala is the centre of a great wheat-growing area.

I walked the length of the main street, out to one end of the town and then back and out to the silo, in search of a hotel and for once was not the object of particular notice. This, I think, was due to the fact that the town was especially crowded by the farmers with their tractors and loads of wheat. There was one tiny hotel whose entrance put even me off, but then at the silo end of town I discovered what appeared to be a brand-new and quite grand hotel. This was firmly closed. It was still only half past eleven so I sought a tea-house, where I had three leisurely teas and asked about the new hotel. The proprietor assured me that it was open and that I would be able to stay there, although he was puzzled as to why I should want to come to Bala at all. After the tea I went back to the hotel and settled on the steps, waiting for someone to come. Word of my presence there, I had no doubt, would get round soon enough.

I was, of course, right. I had hardly settled upon the hotel steps when three youths wandering past along the road first hailed me, then came into the hotel grounds, which in themselves were unusual, for most hotels opened straight on to the road. They were intrigued as to why I had stopped off in Bala. 'There is nothing here', they insisted, 'tourists never stop here; what do you want?'

'Well, I am not a tourist and I just like to see places.'

'But there is nothing to see here.'

'Wheat,' I said, 'the silo, all these farmers bringing in their crops.'

This exposition, simple as it might seem, had taken some time due to language difficulties: it left my audience, now increased to five, totally nonplussed. 'But there is nothing here to do', my first interlocutor repeated: he had some German. We had achieved a sort of stalemate of misunderstanding but at that moment one of them looked at my small bag and, surmising accurately that I had a camera, asked me to take their photograph. So I took a picture of the group and then luckily, before each of them demanded a photograph when I got back to England, the hotel manager arrived. The young men drifted off and the manager took me round the back of the hotel and up an outside staircase to an entrance I had not suspected.

Everything was brand-new: the rooms were clean, the woodwork still gleaming from the recent action of planing, the sheets both clean and new, fresh curtains in place at the windows. But my room only had a small wash-basin, the shower as I discovered later did not yet work, and one WC served the entire floor. I surrendered my passport to the manager and then went to find some lunch.

Normally when I came early enough to a small town, for by this time I was getting into a regular routine, I would spend a good part of the day exploring the surrounding countryside. So I set off along the road which I would take the next day, to be accosted by boys from the high school who had a little English and wanted to test it on me. They knew at once that I was a foreigner, but took a little longer to discover my nationality. Then I left the road and wandered over a knoll to obtain a stunning view across the hills. Below me, perhaps 1 kilometre (half a mile) away, a boy sat on a donkey under a tree guarding his flock of sheep. I descended through a grove of trees down a steep gully until I came to a stream bed – now dry, but lined with thick-leaved trees. It was a marvellous, quiet place and I sat there for an hour writing notes and enjoying the peace. As I had discovered, it was almost impossible to write or read in any public place – a hotel lounge or tea-house, for example – because the mere sight of a book or of me writing would at once bring one or more inquisitive Turks to my side and I would be asked what I was reading or writing, what country I came from, and what I was doing in Turkey. After the third or fourth question I would abandon as hopeless my attempt to read or write and instead surrender myself to conversation.

Back in the town another young man approached to address me in excellent English, with an Australian accent. He was home with his father visiting members of the family but they would shortly return to Sydney, Australia, again. 'See you around', he concluded, proudly using this unmistakable western idiom.

In a large and clean tea-house I settled down for a long relaxation and watched the farmers receiving receipts for the wheat which they had delivered to the silo. The queue of tractors with their trailers of wheat had grown even longer as yet more farmers had arrived in town to add their loads of wheat to the end of the queue. In the afternoon when I was out walking I had seen several great combines working on the hills in the distance. As far as I could gather, though I never asked anybody, the Bala farmers worked on some kind of co-operative basis. Once they had been handed their receipts the farmers were intent on relaxing and soon the escalating noise of conversation was accompanied by the slap of cards or the click of the white wooden pieces used in the game of *Okey* which so intrigued me. Periodically the official from the silo would return to hand out more receipts.

A man joined me at my table. 'What was I doing in Bala?' 'Passing through' or 'just visiting' seem inadequate phrases and they were received, justifiably, with doubt. 'Passing through to where?' Sometimes I would explain that I was on my river trail but, since Bala was some distance away from the Kizil Irmak, that was not the right explanation on this occasion. My inquisitor ordered more tea and asked me how I liked Turkey.

Although earlier the young man had insisted that there was nothing to see or do in Bala he was quite wrong. The people were the chief attraction: farmers relaxing, the tea-house crowded with players, the usual insistently curious individuals who would come to establish my business to their personal satisfaction then drift off to inform their friends about me and later, in return for my having satisfied their curiosity as well as a gesture of courtesy, insist upon paying for a glass of tea. As a rule tourists are so busy seeing places and things that the people of the country in which they are travelling become no more than an animated or animating backdrop to the particular sight being inspected, rather than themselves forming the main attraction. Tourists so often race from place to place. Yet it is extraordinary what just sitting can do for you, and the longer I was in Turkey the more I sat and the more frequently I was approached and questioned. I did not need to work at it: the Turks, I am glad to say, did the work for me. On this occasion, however – the tea-house was one of the largest I could remember up to that point – the farmers who came in gave me interested and curious inspections but left me alone, which was a change.

The Turks are a handsome people although rugged is perhaps a better epithet for the men, and these farmers who as a rule are dark skinned to begin with, had sun-blackened faces. Almost all men above a certain age, perhaps the mid-twenties, sported moustaches and a majority, or so it seemed, sported at least two days' growth of beard as well. More or less without exception the men wore caps, never removed, to cover close-cropped hair, although an increasing number of young men went uncovered and grew their hair longer. A majority of men carried the circles of beads obligatory to Muslims which they worked through their fingers continuously and, for the most part, quite unconsciously. Often, at least in a small town, the men would go around in shirt-sleeves, at any rate in this exceptionally hot weather; otherwise they wore ill-fitting, ill-tailored jackets. When after a lengthy contemplation of this scene I went to pay for my teas the proprietor refused to accept any money: I was a visitor, a guest. So I headed back towards the new hotel but before I could reach it was called over to the first tea-house I had patronised earlier in the day, where I found the man from the hotel, whom I had assumed was the manager. After further teas the two of us returned to the hotel together.

I wanted to do some more writing in my room but almost at once I was disturbed. First my door was thrown open unceremoniously by a young couple I had heard talking in the passage. They apologised but had clearly known I was there and had determined to satisfy their curiosity. Then the manager – it was a municipal hotel I had discovered

– came and insisted I went to sit in the lounge. This was arranged in neat, gleaming cleanliness, virtually unused up to that time. He tried in vain to make the television work but, much to my relief, no image appeared, so he contented himself by providing me – unasked – with a bottle of lukewarm beer (for which I was later charged the high sum of TL 400) and then sitting next to me and engaging me in a long conversation. His only interest was sex and he wanted to make sure I knew about the attractions of Turkish women of doubtful virtue. I was to meet a good deal of this along the way for Turkish men are chauvinistic sexists despite all Atatürk's efforts to emancipate women.

When I had failed to satisfy his curiosity about my intentions with regard to Turkish women I tried to explain that I wished to leave very early in the morning so that I could get in some walking before the heat of the day, and asked him to return my passport and allow me to pay the bill at once. Half an hour of conversation made no difference, not that he did not understand. They had clearly just been instructed in the routine of management and no arguments on my part would persuade him to let me either pay or have my passport that evening. So I walked the now silent town where many trailers of wheat remained in line waiting to be weighed in the morning, for the silo had closed, and I took some photographs.

I had a pleasant supper of doner kebab in the main *lokanta* along the street where I got into conversation with the men at the next table, and when we got stuck – a not infrequent occurrence – someone sent for a schoolboy who had more English and German than any of the men, and he acted as our interpreter. Curiously, I was worried about my passport. I had taken a dislike to the man in the hotel, who was altogether too insistent upon knowing my business in a fashion that was alien to the more usual curiosity which I had come to accept. When I got back I was pleased to find he was gone and in his place was a young man who said he would be there to give me my passport in the morning; he produced a paper with the information from my passport neatly copied on to it. Nowhere else had I met such thoroughness.

# 15

# The Day of the Dogs

I was up and ready to go at six the next morning but the hotel was quite silent, without any sign of the young man. The door on to the veranda and steps, moreover, was locked so that I was a prisoner. I had no idea whether the young man was inside the hotel or would come from outside and after wandering in all the open places and the corridor I resigned myself to waiting and studied my Turkish phrase-book in the deserted lounge. At six-thirty the young man appeared: he had been sleeping in one of the hotel bedrooms. I paid him and retrieved my passport, then he unlocked the door and I set off. I stopped at a small *lokanta* for a bowl of pea soup and a glass of *ayran* – it was already busy – and then at six-forty I began walking. It was cool and I hoped to cover a good many kilometres before the real heat of the day set in. There was quite a bit of traffic on the road, almost all of it consisting of farmers coming into town, and repeatedly I was treated to that Turkish gesture of surprise or interrogation which I met constantly when walking. Whether on the seat of a tractor or driving a lorry or minibus the driver would raise his right hand, splaying his fingers and thumb to form a loose 'cup', and accompanying this gesture with a shrug and facial expression of astonishment: where was I going; there was nothing along that road; why was I walking; no one walked with packs on their backs; was I mad? I would shrug back and sometimes the driver would laugh in understanding at my odd behaviour.

I walked at a steady 5 kilometres (3 miles) an hour and by nine o'clock had covered 12 kilometres (7 miles). I would come to a ridge and then see for miles, and though it was not yet too hot the sun was bright and the air clear, so that distant hills or the valley far below were sharply defined. I came round the steep shoulder of the hill to see a sight I shall never forget. Perhaps 180 metres (200 yards) ahead of me and down the slope of the hill was a huge flock of sheep tightly gathered round a solitary tree. I had heard their bells for some time before I caught sight of them without realising what the sound meant. Standing under the tree leaning on a great stick was the shepherd, while a boy on a donkey circled the flock. Beyond the sheep the hill sloped ever more steeply to the valley far below where trees marked the bed of a river. It was an idyllic, Biblical scene of a kind that could hardly have changed in centuries.

I continued towards the flock enjoying the serenity of this ancient rural picture when seven of the largest sheep detached themselves from the rest and came racing towards me, baying in that deep-throated way which belongs to only the most savage of dogs, and this indeed is what they were. I had forgotten about dogs. These were great Anatolian shepherd dogs, although I was only to discover their breed much later. They were huge with particularly powerful thick shoulders. They wore wide iron collars with 5-cm (2-inch) iron spikes sticking out of them, which perform a dual task; they make it impossible for the dog ever to lay its head flat on the ground to rest, so that they are always watchful with savage tempers to match; and in a fight the spikes, like a weapon, will make the dogs even more formidable than nature and sleeplessness have rendered them already. I stood still, having no weapon. The dogs reached the road and, trained in attack, formed a half-circle round me, growling and snapping. Turning slowly from side to side and saying 'hus, hus' as though I was used to such creatures, I looked in awed and terrified horror at their large blackened teeth which their drawn-back muzzles now revealed. Saliva dripped from their mouths and my apparent unconcern did nothing to quieten them. The shepherd had forced his way through the flock scattering sheep as he came running up the hill towards me; the boy on the donkey was banging his heels into its flanks, forcing it with shrill cries at an unwonted speed up the hillside. I just hoped they would reach me, or rather their dogs, in time. These were now closing in, the nearest no more than 3 metres from me, and I knew that once one made a dash for a bite they would all follow. I thought of Orestes in antiquity, torn to pieces by wild dogs – the thought gave me no comfort. I gave an extra hard stamp with my foot just as the largest and most savage-looking dog moved a pace nearer. The gesture worked, for it backed off snarling and then the shepherd arrived and, not without effort, drove his dogs back. The boy leaped off his donkey and, swishing a stick also, drove them back. Neither of my rescuers took any notice of me whatsoever and though they were now under their control the dogs remained snarling furiously no more than 10 metres behind me as I resumed my walk. I have rarely been so frightened in my life.

One kilometre (half a mile) further on I came up a long slope towards another flock of sheep, also bunched close to the road. I approached cautiously, searching their ranks for dogs but I did not see any. Two shepherds stood talking together; one of these now hailed me and came towards the road and since no dogs materialised I shouted back a greeting and went to shake hands. He eyed my pack with great curiosity; clearly wishing to find out where I was from and where I thought I was going, he brought out of his capacious pocket the filthiest bottle of yoghurt I have ever seen. This he pressed upon me as a refreshment for my journey; it was about half full. I removed the top and swallowed the contents in one great gulp of relief at the absence of dogs as though it were a double whiskey. Then we had a halting conversation with many gestures and pauses. He examined my watch and suggested a swap – his own looked to be *in extremis* – but I declined this offer. Then he asked for a cigarette. My English ones had long been finished and I had taken to carrying a pack of *Samsun* cigarettes, one of the most popular cheap brands, for just such occasions as this. I offered him one but he was disgusted at the sight of them – he had wanted something superior – so we shook hands and I continued upon my way.

I now descended steeply from the long ridge I had been following and began to cross a wide valley, soon finding a suitable place for my first rest of the day. By then I had been walking for nearly three hours without a break, although I was less tired from walking than in need of relaxation after my encounter with the dogs. The thought occurred to me that if I were to perfect the howl of a wolf this would keep them at bay! I cannot imagine how this particular 'defence mechanism' came to mind; luckily I never attempted to put it into practice for as I discovered later these sheepdogs were awarded medals according to the number of wolves they killed.

The sun was now high in the sky and it threatened to be an exceptionally hot day, so after a short pause I continued towards a village. Half-way along I was greeted by a knot of men waiting for a bus. I returned their greeting but continued on my way, although I think they would have liked me to stop and explain myself. At the end of the village the road began to rise sharply towards the hills. On one side the bank had been cut steeply to leave an almost vertical drop of red earth perhaps 3.5 metres (12 feet) high. Above this the grass sloped upwards to a small cottage about 80 metres (about 80 yards) from the road. I gave this a glance and continued on my way but as I did so two huge dogs erupted from the cottage and raced down the grass barking with vicious intent. I thought that, like dogs in England which run to the end of a garden when a stranger passes, they would stop at the steep cut. They didn't even pause but slithered down the almost vertical bank in a swirl of dry dust and came on to the road. One was creamy-white in colour, the other black. They knew their business and went to either side of me. A man had appeared from the cottage above and he was running down the hillside, shouting. Almost at once one of the dogs ran in to bite me on the left thigh. I whirled and it backed off. The other was ready to attack when the man arrived and, snarling, they backed off at his commands from the top of the bank. He took no notice of me. My leg felt quite painful but, despite the sharpness of the dog's teeth, they had not actually penetrated the thick old-fashioned double cotton of my trousers, so I hoped that no saliva had entered my bloodstream. I was now only too aware of the warning of dog bites and rabies which I had received in London.

In Britain, of course, such dogs would soon be put down by court order. Not so in Turkey. I continued my walk, rising steeply out of the valley. Then ahead of me on the stark skyline in black silhouette I saw a solitary dog. It was huge. It did not move but stood like Cerberus at the entrance to Hades as I toiled up the hill. The dog stood, sentinel-like, on one side of the road so I kept to the other. Slowly, wondering what evasive action I could take if attacked, I came abreast of the great creature. Its iron-spiked collar added to its formidable appearance yet it just eyed me, an inspection I warily returned as I walked past; after 100 metres I looked back but it had not moved. Breathing a sigh of relief I breasted a rise only to meet the spectacle of a huge flock of sheep being driven right across the road not 100 metres ahead.

Three dogs came racing towards me barking but the boy on the donkey had his back to me and did not appear to notice what the dogs were doing. I called, urgently, several times before he turned. By then the dogs were standing in a row 15 metres from me, snarling. I took off my belt, which was thick with a strong iron buckle, and curled the end so that I did at least have some weapon. My water-bottle I put in the small bag in which I carried my camera. Then a shepherd whom I had not noticed before came from the other side of the road. He carried a stout stick and was himself of monumental Falstaffian pro-portions. He gave a command and the three dogs backed off. The boy on the donkey, meanwhile, was steadily marshalling the sheep up the hill and away from me. The shepherd came over to greet me. He saw the belt in my hand, curled ready as a weapon, and laughed, indicating his great stick: this is what you need! Then he held out his hand for my belt, which he attempted to put round his waist; the ends would not meet and he roared with delight pointing to his huge stomach. He whistled to his dogs, said goodbye, and once more I was walking on my own.

Scanning the distance for signs of more sheep I put my belt back on and continued walking, but shortly afterwards a car came by and stopped abruptly. There were three men in it who insisted upon giving me a lift as far as Karakacili. Then I was back on the river again.

# 16

# Kaman

There is a lovely stretch of the Kizil Irmak by the little village of Koprukoy. The river passes through a rock gorge and an old bridge with isolated arches in its structure set far above the water-level looks as though it has been carved from the rocks of the gorge behind it. Here the river was deep and clear and it was one of the only occasions when I swam in it. Two small boys appeared from the village; they wanted their photographs taken. I obliged and then some men wandered up and we sat on the river-bank talking before I resumed my walk. Later I diverged from the river, for there was no track, and took the road to Kaman.

Kaman turned out to be an exciting little town. I arrived quite early in the day for though I had set out to walk I was given a lift – unsolicited – by a German-speaking Turk. He was intrigued by what I was doing and was so busy questioning me on the ride that I missed the scenery of the 20 kilometres (12 miles) before the town. I got a room in the Hotel Aydin and then explored the town, which was bustling with activity and preparations for market the next day. I sat for an hour by a blue tiled pond under a spreading ash tree in a pleasant tea-garden and was left to myself, which was certainly a change.

I watched a repulsive crippled beggar making a slow round of the garden. His legs were askew, fixed in an awful bandiness from some childhood deficiency so that he was obliged to heave himself along, half a step at a time, his shuffling and grunting preceding him as a warning of his approach, which was as painful for each person he confronted as it was for the beggar himself. Everyone gave something – and though Turks could be generous to the down-and-out they could also be quite indifferent (I have seen a beggar go round an entire tea-garden and get nothing) – and I got the impression that his repulsive aspect worked heavily in his favour. The men gave him something so

77

that he would move on; he knew it, too. Once he had received a contribution he took about 30 seconds to shift himself into gear again before he was ready to lurch away. I do not like beggars, partly because they induce in me a sense of guilt at my own good fortune, and partly because when I do succumb to their blandishments and give I almost invariably feel that I have been conned and have given to the wrong kind of beggar, one who is not truly deserving. Crippled beggars make me especially uncomfortable; they always seem to have the advantage and they trade upon it outrageously.

Back in the hotel I examined my leg; the dog bite had been throbbing all morning and had produced an ugly bruise whose skin had broken so that my trousers now had a patch of matching blood on them. I thought again of rabies but then recalled Oliver Goldsmith's lines:

> The dog, to gain some private ends,
> Went mad and bit the man
>
> The man recover'd of the bite,
> The dog it was that died.

This doggerel gave me an immediate sense of satisfaction and I was able to put aside the thought of rabies and relax.

On one side of the main road Kaman's narrow streets went sharply up and down hills, and overlooking a picturesque square was a first-floor *restoran* where I sat by a window drinking beer. I came to like Turkish beer, especially when I had been walking. On this occasion I sat for several hours, had lunch, then more beer and wrote notes. For once I was left to do this in peace although when I went to leave the waiter brought me another beer with the compliments of a man on the other side of the dining-room, so I joined him for a talk. On such occasions I tried to apportion motives for hospitality: how much was it traditional Turkish hospitality, the determination to make a stranger feel welcome; and how much was the gesture designed to entrap me into providing information? It is difficult not to answer innocent questions about who you are, where you come from, what you are doing, and why when you have just accepted a drink from a total stranger. The Turks are cunning in this respect.

After the beer I went shopping. The market stalls were crowded into several of the small winding streets, where I took photographs and was frequently asked questions as I wandered slowly from stall to stall. Then I found a German-speaking man and told him the object of my search: a walking-stick to keep the sheepdogs at bay. He was delighted at this and took me to a shop of a friend, where tea was promptly produced while a boy was sent off to get a stick for me. I told the story of the dogs to a highly appreciative audience who appeared to be more on the side of the dogs than of me. The boy returned with a selection of three sticks for me to choose from and I picked the stoutest. It cost TL 2,000 (just over 1 pound sterling) and from then on I carried it with me everywhere just in case.

Back in the tea-garden under the ash tree I got into conversation with three men who asked me why I carried a walking-stick, so once more I told the story of the dogs. They, too, thought it an excellent joke. Two of them spoke some German and I found, as I did again and again, that my somewhat limited German was quite invaluable. It did at least enable me to get by just about anywhere in the country.

I wandered to the outskirts of the town and watched youths playing football. The Turks were mad about football and often when they discovered that I was English would come out with the name of a team such as Arsenal: they had the idea that we were the best players in the world!

One of the trials of being a foreigner in such a town was the attraction I always exercised for groups of small children, who would follow me endlessly, repeating the only English they knew: '*What is your name? My name is* ... *Hello!*' It could be extremely irritating, but to show annoyance was fatal. Then they would laugh and redouble their chants: '*What is your name,*' if necessary from a safe distance.

I returned to my lunch and beer *restoran* for an evening meal, regarding it as an establishment of the first class. It had green felt table-cloths and clean linen napkins, while a packet of cigarettes was delivered to the table already opened. The clientele clearly came for a slow relaxing meal and drinks. I spent a long evening there and several people came over to greet me and inquire where I came from and ask where I was going, but then they left me alone.

That night I had a nightmare: I was gazing up a beautiful green hill at a flock of pure white sheep when these all began to race down the hill towards me and as they did so turned into giant dogs with spiked collars. I woke in a sweat just as they reached me.

The wisdom-tooth on my lower right jaw had been slowly loosening ever since my arrival in Turkey; the day of the dogs had loosened it, sympathetically, another notch so that it now fairly rattled in my mouth although its roots were sufficiently deep that I felt it would still take some time before it worked itself free.

The early morning call to prayer broke through my half-sleep when it was still dark; here in Kaman it was gentle and seemed more like an invitation to go back to sleep again. Later, I spent an hour wandering through the market, which filled several streets and was one of the best I had encountered. Apart from a great range of fruit and vegetables there was a whole street of household goods, clothes and farm implements including iron spiked collars for sheepdogs. I was frequently questioned and took a number of photographs.

Back on the main street I was making my way to the tea-garden when I was hailed from a car by a man with an Australian accent. He insisted that I wait for him at a little roadside café while he dropped off the other occupants of his car: he would return to me in ten minutes, he said. So I drank peach nectar and waited. He soon returned, a man full of himself: he had lived in Australia for years and was just back visiting. He had taken six months off but would go back to Australia in October. He had a house here in Kaman, which was his home-town, and his mother looked after it – he would take me now to see it. He would also pay for my drink, but by the time he had come back I had had two peach nectars. I told him this and though he began to insist it was only for form, and I paid.

We drove to his house, which was on the hill over the town. A woman, I think a relative, brought us coffee – Nescafé – and my host then told me more of his life. He had been in Australia 18 years, had put his hand to a number of jobs, but was vague as to what he now did – some kind of business – and his children were all in Australia, his sons having married Australian wives. The house was over-furnished in garish style but he was inordinately proud of it and took me round to inspect every room.

For once I had met someone who was so concerned to tell me his own life story that he omitted to subject me to the usual cross-examination about my doings, which was both a relief and a change. Ismet was his name, and he was determined that I should know just how well he had done. I met other Turks like Ismet, those who had made good in Germany or somewhere else and were both proud of their achievement and yet at the same time possessed of a kind of inferiority for they knew, even if they could not articulate the knowledge, that they were only on the edge of a new life style. Sometimes in my presence such people would be aggressive towards other Turks who had not been abroad to work so as to demonstrate their superiority and to make the point that they were on a par with me, the stranger who came from one of the rich lands like the one in which they had made good. It was part of a pervasive pattern in a country of great poverty where the ambition of so many was to emigrate, at least for part or all of their working lives, and make wealth to bring back home.

# 17

# Kirşehir

From Kaman the main road runs to Kirşehir while a smaller, parallel road runs alongside the Kizil Irmak, which is at a distance of about 20 kilometres (12 miles) from the main road. A great dam has turned a long stretch of the river into a lake and at the head of this, where the river has returned to its normal size, lies the little village of Kesikopru. The remains of an ancient dilapidated caravanserai stand at the outskirts of the village, which once was a place of far greater importance than it is today. I inspected this and peered through the closed gates into the ruined interior behind the massive walls, which I believe date from the twelfth century.

A magnificent bridge of eleven arches crosses the river but as I approached it a great flock of sheep began to disgorge from the end nearest to me so I stood well to one side to let them and their attendant dogs pass. The shepherd rode a donkey and cracked a whip, which I considered as an alternative weapon for future defence. A large iron-collared dog did turn to snarl at me but I stood still, grasping my walking stick, and he went back to his business. When the sheep had been driven up the hill behind the village I crossed the bridge and took some photographs. Not far away was a second, modern bridge which I imagine had been constructed in relation to the dam downstream. Great trucks kept crossing it both ways and disappearing over a ridge. Under its shade, on the same side as I now found myself, was another flock of sheep attended only by a small boy, but he was accompanied by two great dogs so I kept my distance.

Back across the bridge on a knoll above the road was a small gendarme post. These were to be found in most towns but not generally in small villages: I supposed it had something to do with the dam. As I passed, one of the soldiers hailed me from above so I went up to visit. As a rule such posts were immaculately kept and this was no exception. The small barracks was surrounded by a garden and the three men who appeared to make up its total complement – a full corporal, a lance-corporal and a private – were relaxing in an elegant little garden-house covered by vines. They were drinking tea and the soldier was dispatched to find another glass for me. None had any language other than Turkish so after a few tries I brought out my small dictionary. They enjoyed this and I spent an hour and a half with the three of them asking questions to which they provided answers with the help of the dictionary. We examined the newspaper, in which there was a picture of the Queen Mother, who had just celebrated her eighty-seventh birthday. The Turks like the British Royal Family, and appear to be mesmerised by Mrs Thatcher.

'You are hungry?' the corporal asked. I was, as it happened, and said so. The corporal gave a command and the private disappeared into the barracks. We continued our dictionary conversation, which was mainly an attempt by me at translating some of the articles in the newspaper. The two corporals got so excited that they would grab the dictionary from one another as they sought to explain things. Princess Margaret had visited Istanbul, a Saudi Arabian had attempted to assassinate the Ayatollah and Gadaffi had married again. Then the soldier returned with a meal for me: meat stew with tomatoes and green peppers, goat's cheese and bread. It was excellent. After that we had some more tea and then I took their photographs.

I now took the road to Kırşehir which was about 20 kilometres (12 miles) distant. I had not gone more than 2 or 3 when a tractor and trailer came along and gave me a lift. The trailer was piled high with hay, on to which I clambered to join a man and a woman. The man spoke some German but was not very talkative, which allowed me to enjoy the drive. The road was straight and the driver took us along at a spanking pace; it was a marvellously cool way to travel despite the heat for the speed was enough to create a pleasant breeze and from the top of the loaded trailer I got a magnificent view across the rolling countryside. They dropped me in the dusty outskirts of Kırşehir.

There are curious contradictions about the way Turks behave towards strangers. Their friendliness and hospitality is always matched by an abiding inquisitiveness but also, sometimes, by an odd indifference. On this occasion when I got down from the trailer and went to shake hands with the driver and thank him for the lift he could hardly wait to be off: he gave a shrug and a perfunctory handshake and was away again. He was happy to help and would have done so for anyone, was the implication of that shrug. I was, perhaps, as a foreigner, marginally more interesting than a Turk would have been but that was all.

I had to walk several kilometres along a dusty road before reaching the centre of Kirşehir, which is quite a large town. An enormous ditch had been dug along the road for new sewerage. I came to a tiny shop sporting a Fanta sign; three people sat under a tree on the opposite side of the road, clearly intrigued by my appearance. I went into the shop, which was empty, but the woman under the tree came across to serve me and I had a cold drink. Unusually, she was ready to be talkative and asked questions which a man who had now joined us translated into German. Then I continued into Kirşehir.

I forgot about time in Turkey. In Britain we murder time, doing everything according to the clock so that time rules our lives, although we no longer understand how to enjoy it. I am a stickler for time: I expect people to arrive on the dot and, for example, if someone is coming to see me at six o'clock and is a minute or more late I stand at my window surveying the street below and wondering – furiously – what has caused him or her to be late. In Turkey I found myself enjoying time – just time to be, not time in which something had to be done. It was an exhilarating experience. I would eat or drink tea and then think, or not think, for I did not have to be off, I had no schedule to keep. So, if I felt like it, I would sit contemplating, endlessly.

Kirşehir possessed three famous mosques, one of which had once been an observatory, and I spent the late afternoon visiting them. The town was founded in ancient times but became famous in the Middle Ages as the centre of the Ahi Brotherhood, a Muslim sect which advanced new social and moral ideals. The thirteenth-century Cacabey Mosque which was once an astronomical observatory is a splendid example of Seljuk architecture. The stone is heavy, the proportions perfect, the entire surface of the floor covered with a wealth of Turkish carpets and rugs. One small mosque was situated on a citadel-like hill above the town where there was also a tea-garden. Like every tea-house or tea-garden this one had a television set which was constantly at work. The products included a high proportion of video melodramas which the sets were more likely to be showing than television programmes. While I sat looking across the distant country most of the other customers were glued to a television drama among the trees. On my way down the steps from this steep place I stopped by one of the boys with a weighing machine: I found that I had lost 5.4 kg (12 lb) since I had set out from Bafra.

# 18

# Haçibektaş Interlude

My next stop after Kirşehir was at Haçibektaş, a small town high in the hills, famous for the Islamic thinker, Haçi Bektaş Veli, who lived here in the thirteenth century. He migrated to Turkey from Iran during the Seljuk period and was the founder of the Bektashi Order. His saying, 'Nations which do not educate their women cannot progress', was one of great enlightenment for his time and is well worth repeating in the Islamic world of today.

I arrived in the little town of Mucur by *dolmus* from Kirşehir, having carried on a conversation for 22 kilometres (13 miles) in English and Turkish with the man seated beside me. Neither understood a word the other said but my companion was so delighted with this process that he insisted upon paying my fare and then helped me find a taxi to Haçibektaş. This I shared with four others at a cost of TL 600. When we arrived in the centre of Haçibektaş I broke one of my firm rules: instead of walking round the town in search of a hotel I allowed myself to be persuaded by the taxi-driver that the only hotel was the rather smart establishment we had already passed on the outskirts of the town. He assumed that as a foreigner I would want the best and Haçibektaş, as I was to discover, was something of a special tourist attraction. So I walked back down and up a hill to a hotel 'Turist' – it called itself a Hotel Village House – and asked for a room. At first they said there was nothing available but when I pressed they agreed to let me have a room just for that night. I was curious as to why they showed such reluctance as the place seemed almost deserted; later I discovered that a large party had booked all the rooms for the following night: they were coming for the annual festival celebrating the life and works of Haçi Bektaş Veli. My room was far better appointed than any I had been in for some time and had a good shower with hot water, which made a change. I made my way to the dining-room for a slow lunch.

Half-way through my meal a substantial, balding gentleman approached my table and greeted me by name: 'Mr Arnold?' he inquired on a rising note, 'the writer?' This would have been quite remarkable flattery except that I had filled in my occupation in the hotel register. He introduced himself as a professor from Ankara University who had come to Haçibektaş for the Islamic festival which began the next day. He assumed I was there for the same reason and, moreover, was going to write about it. He was accompanied by an American wife and his sister, who alone of the three spoke little English but was of dark, compelling beauty. They joined me at my table.

We had a pleasant conversation but my new friend found a certain difficulty in hiding his disappointment when he discovered that I was there by accident, had known nothing of the Islamic or historic importance of Haçibektaş and would not be staying for the festival nor writing about it. He was one of the organisers of an academic event which was to take place during the festival and, I suspect, having cornered me in my capacity as a writer in the hope that I would say nice things about his organisation did not quite know how next to proceed. I did not really sympathise with his plight and waited to see how he would handle it. His American wife came to his rescue and asked what I was doing in Haçibektaş and, for that matter, Turkey. So I told them of the journey I was making and, since it was a recent experience, about my encounters with the sheepdogs. It was the professor who informed me that they were given medals according to the number of wolves they had killed.

He was intrigued that I intended to go to Zara: 'That is right in the hills', he said, as though it represented a remoteness beyond his normal interests. He told me that the people of that region moved up into the hills with their sheep during the summer and had an interesting pattern of migration back and forth between their villages and their summer pastures. We got on to the fact that I wished to write a book and, while showing polite interest – far less, I felt, than had I been about to write up his festival – he said that the Turks do not like people to write books about them: what they do not know is not worth knowing. It was an arrogant dismissal although he made the point in a jovial light-hearted fashion. I left soon afterwards and went to visit the town.

The town centre had grown up round the complex of the dervish convent or *dergah* which now houses a museum. It was an interesting architectural mixture dating from the thirteenth century onwards, and frequently restored. The town was fairly crowded with Turkish rather than foreign tourists who had come for the festival. Apart from the museum and mosque there was a charming little market selling the usual abundance of melons and water-melons, which were heaped in great yellow and green piles, while stalls displayed a range of small onyx ornaments for which the area is famous. In the mosque I sat for a while beside a Turk who told me something of its history in halting German. Then I returned to the hotel to write notes and have an afternoon rest.

I walked back into the town before dinner and was greeted just as I came to the top of the hill by a man who had a smattering of English. He had about him something of the air of a stage villain. 'Come and see my store', he invited. This turned out to be a liquor warehouse and for a small town which was also an Islamic holy place it was extremely wellstocked, not only with a large consignment of wines and *raqi*, but with whisky and vodka as well. My friend spread a large map on his desk and I showed him where I had been and where I intended to go. He had been drinking and was in high spirits; each explanation demanded the use of German, English and my dictionary. Then he produced a bottle of wine: it was '79 vintage, a full-bodied red but a bit sweet for my taste. He drank it like schnapps: we each had a small glass which he filled to the brim and then we tossed back the contents in a single motion. When the bottle was half empty I began to feel the effects of this particular way of consuming wine, while my host, I am convinced, had already drunk a quantity of beer. Then I noticed a curious bulge over his stomach. He followed my gaze, laughed, swayed to his feet and extracted from under his shirt an enormous pistol. 'I don't need this any more', he said, and wove his way across the room to a safe in which he deposited his weapon. He returned and refilled our glasses. I had difficulty in escaping from him and only managed to do so when the bottle was empty.

Back in the hotel dining-room the professor led in a group of ten including a very important bearded man who was clearly a senior academic figure. He was treated by the others with a deference which he brushed aside, though expecting that it would continue to be offered. This turned out to be the case. My professor introduced me across the room and since at lunch-time we had talked of eating together exhibited a certain embarrassment. The bearded academic looked upon me with no favour at all so after a few courteous bows I resumed my seat and left them to their academic reflections. It was an important occasion, a middle-class Turkish dinner, women for once on a par with men, which was something I did not often see in the places which I was in the habit of frequenting.

That night was remarkably cold. My loose wisdom-tooth, which had begun to rattle in my mouth, finally worked itself free. I looked upon my brief stop here as the 'Haçibektaş interlude'. My bill in the morning came to the astronomical figure of TL 31,000 (22 pounds sterling): though a modest sum according to international tourist standards it was phenomenal in terms of my normal hotel outlays. The food had been pleasant and the hot shower a treat yet somehow I saw Haçibektaş as a kind of diversion, partly because it represented a total change from my normal small, cheap hotel; and partly because the middle-class, rather self-conscious academics had been less than certain how to take me. Bearded and roughly dressed, behaving neither like an academic (writer) nor a tourist, I must have seemed a strangely outlandish figure and they found themselves at something of a loss. For my part I had felt far more at home gulping back the sweet red wine with the man with the gun than listening to the professor talk about the peasants in the hills round Zara whom I doubt he had ever been near.

*St Sofia, Istanbul*

*Hills – looking down on the Kolay dam*

*A familiar sight: water-melons*

*View of mountains from Haçilar, across the river valley*

*Old house with storks, Haçilar*

*The matriarch, Sarimbey*

*The market at Kamam*

*The Kizil Irmak passing through a gorge*

*Twelfth-century mosque, Kirşehir*

*Soldiers at a guard post, Kesikopru*

*The town of Uçhisar from the rock citadel, Cappadocia*

*Tea-garden, Uçhisar*

*Goreme – some of the famous rock caves in Cappadocia*

*Lion gate, Hattusas*

*Two policemen, who chased the author
into the hills, at Suşehri*

*Wheat drying on the banks of the river and women washing clothes, Zara*

*Dye factory, Tokat*

*Children, Tokat*

*The Yeşil Irmak at Amasya, with one of its famous water-wheels*

*On the river at Çarşamba*

*The Yeşil Irmak dam – blue waters – at Ayvacik*

*The author on a donkey in the hills near Kosçu*

# 19

# Cappadocia

The little town of Avanos is situated on the southernmost bend of the Kizil Irmak and with Gülsehir, which is a few kilometres downstream to the west, it marks the northern limit of the astonishing area of Cappadocia, which is riddled with the troglodyte dwellings, Byzantine churches and monasteries carved out of the soft volcanic rocks that have turned the countryside into a kind of fairyland. For a thousand years of the Byzantine Empire the region was a centre for monks. When the Empire contracted the rock caves became refuges from marauding enemies such as the invading Arabs of the ninth century. Only with the coming of the Mongols and Turks did its significance decline as all Anatolia fell under Muslim rule. Even so, some of the churches functioned until the present century. Then, at the end of the Greek-Turkish war which followed World War 1 the Greek Christians of Anatolia were deported to Greece as part of an exchange of minorities.

Only during the present century has the existence of these rock dwellings and Byzantine churches become widely known, and only since World War 2 have large numbers of people been able to visit them. They are amongst Turkey's major tourist attractions. Gülsehir and Avanos are both on the Kizil Irmak and on my direct walking route but I decided to detour south and make Nevşehir my headquarters for several days while I explored the region.

The small towns of Ürgüp and Goreme to the east of Nevşehir and the country round them contain the most famous of all the rock churches, although the whole region is riddled with them. The wall-paintings in these churches comprise the greatest museum of Byzantine Christian art in existence, covering a period which begins with the early Christians of the sixth century and ends only with the establishment of Ottoman rule in the thirteenth century. The extraordinary, soft rock is volcanic, the result of what must once have been a mighty eruption of Mount Erciyes, 50 kilometres (30 miles) further east still. The porous stone has been ceaselessly eroded and fashioned by the elements and rivers into the present landscape of fanciful turrets, castles, crags and valleys. Some of the rock cones which the Turks call fairy chimneys have black capitals balanced on top like odd-shaped mushrooms. It is possible to wander endlessly in these fantastic valleys whose colours range from brick red through light yellow to a brilliant white under the sharp clear sun. And since earliest times the people of Cappadocia have cut into the soft rocks to make homes, monasteries, chapels or fortresses into which they could retreat in times of danger. Many of the villages of the area are a mixture of rock caves and houses which have been built of the local stone so that the two blend together and, sometimes, it is impossible to distinguish clearly one from the other.

The red in the Kizil Irmak comes from the volcanic clays of Cappadocia. Avanos, an enchanting little town built up a steep rock side, looks down on the river, which at this point is broad and flows gently. Avanos is famous for dozens of small potteries, some claiming to use the same methods that were employed in antiquity, which now cater principally for tourists. In the ancient world the clay from Avanos was exported to potters all over the eastern Mediterranean.

I shared a taxi from Nevşehir to Avanos with three Spaniards and we got there early in the morning, ahead of the day's influx of tourists. Though the town is enchanting it has become a tourist-trap full of cafés, displays of onyx, potters insisting that they will make something special for you, brilliant carpets and rugs hanging out to catch the eye. I, of course, was a traveller, not a tourist, which is quite different. I inspected several potteries and in one was invited to watch while my French-speaking host fashioned an elegant little pot on his wheel. He insisted that the method of working which he employed had not altered in 2,000 years though I had my doubts; nevertheless I purchased two tiny pots from him – so small and light that they would make no difference to my load, take no space and not break. Then I walked up the steep village streets on to the hilltop beyond. Twice I had to brace myself and raise my stick as marauding village dogs of the larger, more savage variety approached me in hostile fashion. But I was getting used to them. Back in the little town centre I sat in a tea-garden and in the inevitable conversation with the men at the next table once more raised the subject of dogs. 'Yes, yes,' they chortled, 'we do have fierce dogs in our villages.' I alone, I decided, took the damned brutes seriously. Perhaps that was why they always wanted to attack me.

I walked along the bank of the Kizil Irmak and came across a large party of Turks having a picnic. They greeted me but did not invite me to join them, for which I was grateful since I wanted to be alone. Further along the river-bank under a great tree I sat smoking and contemplating the smooth-flowing water, here quite blue for a change.

Goreme is the centre of the rock caves and chapels, most of which are now easily accessible and open to the public. That was part of the trouble. The place was crawling with tourists, bused in from far afield: German groups, Japanese groups, French groups, English groups, Italian groups, even a Turkish group, though it managed to maintain a certain inconspicuous anonymity. One great amphitheatre of rocks and caves makes up the Goreme museum: a collection of cave dwellings, chapels and monastic quarters which once formed a flourishing town hidden deep in its fantastic valley. Often the openings can only be approached up steep flights of steps carved into the rock face and the entrances could be closed by great rocks in times of danger. The most famous of these chapels are the Church of the Sandal and the Church of the Apple. Some of the Byzantine paintings have been defaced, not by ancient iconoclasts or Muslim fanatics abominating the rival faith, but by modern vandals who have inscribed their names and dates across the paintings or simply scribbled all over them in childish fashion.

By the time I had explored this museum, slipping into caves between the organised groups, I found the whole place had become stifling. I suppose the tourists themselves cannot help it but any pleasure or possibility of contemplating an ancient mystery is totally destroyed when 20 earnest Japanese crowd on one side of you while an arrogant French professor delivers a lecture to his group on the other side. So I left Goreme and walked up and down steep hills until I came to the little town of Ortahisar.

Uçhisar is the most spectacular of the Cappadocian villages. Its houses cluster round a huge rock honeycombed with caves, which rises above the landscape and forms a landmark visible from miles away. Ortahisar also clusters round a rock citadel. It is smaller than Uçhisar but just as picturesque. I sat on a platform café below the rock citadel overlooking the little town square to drink a beer. The weather was quite cool and overcast for a change so that I hurried with my drink and then ascended the citadel, climbing from one cave to another by steep iron ladders which have been added for the benefit of tourists, some of whom I found half-way up, having abandoned the struggle to get to the top. From each cave the view became more exciting, while from the top it was possible to see for miles over the eroded white hills with deep clefts of green valleys between them spreading out from the citadel like a fan. I had lunch in a pleasant little café in the square and then idled away an hour under the trees of a tea-garden.

While drinking my tea I watched a thickset youth being tormented by some small boys; he was 'simple' and his reactions to the taunts flung at him always came too late. He picked up a ridiculously flimsy flower stem and rushed at the boys brandishing it as though it were a whip. They ran off across the square hooting with laughter. The youth returned to the centre of the tea-garden where he sat down as though contented, the fracas of a few moments before already forgotten. The Turks, I found, except for small boys, were nice to mad or simple people. I saw quite a few such characters and almost invariably they were treated with a friendly tolerance. On more than one occasion, moreover, when I witnessed someone behave oddly, Turks who saw me made a point of coming to point out that he was harmless – as in Çorum where I had seen a small, thickset man of immense muscular strength rushing, again and again, head foremost into a wall. It did not appear to do him any damage.

One guidebook describes Nevşehir as a 'characterless modern town'; I did not find it anything of the sort. So much depends upon mood and what you are looking for. As I walked into the centre of the town with my pack on my back a young man fell in beside me to greet me in German. I asked him about hotels and when I made plain that I wanted a cheap one he led me to the Sunar which cost a mere TL 1,500 (1 pound sterling) a night. After settling in I set out, as usual, to explore the town.

Nevşehir is dominated by a citadel crowned with a ruined fort of Seljuk origin. Small, winding streets, some so steep that the roof of one house ends level with the front door of the next house up the hill, eventually open out on to the rough hillside below the fort. A solitary porter at the entrance charged me TL 100 and then I wandered in the deserted interior of the crumbling fort and walked its walls to look down on the town below and across the countryside to what appeared to be a nearby hill village, a mixture of houses and caves.

On my way back down to the town I took a picture of a group of children. This was always easy to do, as they pestered me endlessly to have their photos taken. While I was arranging them, however, I saw at the bottom of the narrow hill where I stood, perhaps 100 metres below me, a group of women sitting talking. They each wore head-scarves and I determined to take their picture as well. I changed the lens and so as not to alert them as to my intentions pretended to focus upon a distant building. But they were not fooled at all. One shouted at me, another waved her arms and a third got up and began to walk hastily away. I took the picture quickly. I was, of course, quite wrong to do so; normally I never take pictures without permission of the subject, a rule I have long kept in all my travels. But in Turkey, despite Atatürk and liberation, many women still wear at least partial purdah and, while men fall over themselves to be photographed, women on their own generally refuse to be taken and resent or repel even the suggestion that they might pose for a camera.

In the upper part of the town near the main bus station I sat in the open for a meal. The cafés in the square appeared to be frequented solely by tourists, mainly young people, so I moved off to inspect the market. This was teeming with activity and packed with produce: melons, beans, peppers, tomatoes, aubergines, apples, pears, grapes, peaches, potatoes. I took a photograph of a lorry stacked high with deep purple aubergines. The eighteenth-century Kursunlu Mosque is a beautifully proportioned building with a finely decorated dome roof inside. Nearby is an elegant library. Then I entered the Turkish baths, which are centuries old, and was shown all over them by a friendly attendant. I was, I suppose, now being a tourist, but at least I was being one on my own and at leisure. I found a pub: it was a businesslike place in which customers purchased tickets for drinks at the door. I failed to understand this and simply went to the centre – there was no room to sit – where I was brought a drink anyway. It was not a place frequented by tourists – that was very clear – so that I was the object of considerable interest. After a while some men left and I took a seat to find myself opposite a two-fingered drunk who leered questions at me with increasing ferocity as he discovered that we had no common language. I offered him a cigarette but as I did not want one myself he became offended. In the end I gave him my pack and left.

Still obsessed by the possibility of fresh attacks from dogs on my walks I purchased some strips of leather from a harness shop. These I plaited into a whip as an additional weapon. I found that with much practice I could make it give a reasonably sharp crack but somehow doubted that it would be of much real use in the event of an attack.

One evening in Nevşehir I walked out of the town towards the hill village which I had seen from the citadel. I had asked about this in the tourist office but had been assured that there was no rock village anywhere near. None the less, I determined to explore. On the outskirts of the town I cut across some rough ground, pursued as usual by small children calling: 'Hello, *what is your name?*' After negotiating a stream I walked up a steep hill into a village many of whose houses were built out of, into or round the steep rock face that rose behind the main square. A teenage boy with reasonable French offered to show me round and together we climbed through the little streets and out above the village. There an apparently endless cemetery stretched through the long grass across a flat hilltop. We took a longer, less steep road back. It was an enchanting place. A tea-garden occupied a terrace overlooking the village square and my guide insisted upon treating me to tea before I returned to Nevşehir. Perhaps the man in the tourist office had wanted to dissuade me from visiting it because the local people did not wish to be disturbed by tourists.

On one occasion when I was leaving the hotel I found the German-speaking youth who had led me to it on my arrival sitting in the tiny foyer. He insisted upon coming with me. I told him I wished to explore the town so he guided me in ways I did not wish to go and then, after no more than five minutes of walking, suggested we needed a rest. So we found a tea-house and he made a great to-do ordering tea, and drawing attention to himself in the process. Almost every table was occupied with men playing cards or the game of *Okey* and in either case always slapping their cards or pieces down on the tables as hard as possible so that there was a constant volley of such sound. My host asked if I played dominoes and then went to fetch a set: these were very small, fine brass pieces. I had not played dominoes in years and was not sure how to do so any more but managed quite well, for at one point I almost won. The game was quickly over and my guide did not wish to play any more. Instead he produced a box of pills and swallowed several. He explained that they were for his nerves – I should think he was no more than 19 or 20, but he was clearly in a state of high tension. He explained that he was home on a visit from Frankfurt where his father worked and he went to high school. He seemed quite close to a nervous breakdown.

He was a potential casualty of a different culture clash and, I suspect, was typical of quite a few of the younger generation of Turks who have been partly brought up in Germany where, over the last 20 years, their parents have gone to profit from the German economic miracle. Much of the sophistication which he had attempted to demonstrate for my benefit was a veneer that had come close to cracking when he returned to his Turkish roots. He wanted desperately to show that he had made a cultural leap, while in his heart he had no certainty at all. 'Let us go', he said abruptly, and he called loudly to the proprietor to pay for our tea and then led me back to the hotel. I did not wish to go in so said goodbye and went to do what I had intended in the first place, leaving him standing bemused on the hotel steps. Much later when I returned the hotel proprietor and another young man who spoke English apologised to me on behalf of the German-speaking youth. They said he was odd, perhaps ill, and were relieved that I had not minded his strange behaviour. Partly they were protecting him – they were, I think, perceptively aware of his problem – and partly they did not want to upset me, a stranger. More than once I encountered young Turks who had become partly deracinated and were no longer certain where they belonged.

I dined in my favourite restaurant that evening and after I had finished a bottle of wine and was considering what to have next a large *raqi* was sent to me with compliments from a neighbouring table, where six men and an attendant small boy were enjoying themselves. Later they sent grapes to accompany the *raqi* and then a peach, brought by the little boy who was delighted to be entrusted with such a task. One of the men came over to ask me something – I think to join them – but I declined so he kissed me on both cheeks and returned to his companions. When I was ready for a second *raqi* I felt obliged to order it surreptitiously so that my neighbours would not feel it incumbent upon them to supply me a second time.

# 20

# Kayseri and the Mountain

I found the city of Kayseri a delight: it has historical monuments in plenty, a marvellous, lively covered bazaar and endless carpet touts. These gentlemen sidle up to beguile you in the streets, inquiring how you like Turkey and whether they can be of help. They do this in good English or German and then, when their friendliness has lowered your guard, whisk you off to the 800-year-old *Bedesten* which is the centre of the carpet-selling business. In the distance, one of the grandest sights of Turkey, lies snow-capped Erciyes, Mount Argaeus of antiquity.

I came to Kayseri from Nevşehir. It lies south of the river and Erciyes is a further 25 kilometres (15 miles) south again. I wanted to visit both. Kayseri is at the centre of ancient Anatolian trade routes and has long been a city of significance, fought over through the ages and today one of the most important in Turkey. Originally known as Mazarca, it was the capital of Cappadocia, but a sycophantic king who only retained his title courtesy of the conquering Romans renamed it Caesarea to honour Augustus, and Kayseri is a corruption of that.

Kayseri was the only city in all my journey in which I was tackled by people as though I were a tourist, but that was by the carpet salesmen and they pursued everyone. This is the centre of the carpet and kilim rug producing area and I was to spend hours in the upper balcony of the old *bedesten* being shown a wide selection of rugs, most of which I would happily have purchased had I been able to afford them. They were priced at a quarter of what would be paid in London.

I often sought the quiet of mosques. It was relaxing to sit cross-legged in a dark corner contemplating the rich fabric of endless Turkish rugs that covered the entire floor space. Turkish men who came to pray would select their own isolated spot and carry out their devotions oblivious to anyone else. I would be given a brief, passing inspection but that was all. Sometimes I entered a teaching mosque where a group of boys, or several groups in different corners, would cluster cross-legged round a *haji* for instruction, or individual men would sit, the Koran held open on their knees, reciting aloud. The interior of the thirteenth-century Huant mosque was one of the most beautiful I visited.

Massive Seljuk fortifications on the south side of the old medieval town are impressive reminders of a military people who preceded the Ottoman Turks, and scattered about the city are the conical-roofed individual tombs of the wealthy and powerful, also from the Seljuk period. I walked to the Archaeological Museum on the outskirts of the city and was startled by the Geordie accents of three young men engrossed by its classical treasures, and somehow not tourists at all. On my return from the museum I entered the covered bazaar and at once a smooth, slightly flash man fell in beside me: German? English? French? Could he help me? 'English', I replied.

'Can your speak German?' he asked.

'Yes, a little.'

'You are looking for something?'

'Yes, a whip to keep the dogs at bay.' This startled him.

'Perhaps I can show you round the bazaar, I should like to be of help.'

'Why not. Thank you very much.'

So he did – it was my first visit to the bazaar – guiding me inexorably towards his target. We entered the old *Bedesten*, which was a place of noise and bustle and business. Beautiful bright-coloured kilim rugs hung over the balustrade of the upper balcony. I took a photograph. 'You are interested in our Turkish carpets?' inquired my guide. He was cunning, this one.

'Yes indeed,' I said. 'Let us go up and see some, then.' We did so. I spent an hour with him as, one by one, he laid rugs and kilims at my feet until he had built up a pile before me. But I was not buying that day and said I would come back. His face fell and his German became faster as he grew more excited at the thought that a customer was about to slip through his fingers. He was not the boss man, only one of the roving salesmen who set upon strangers. He was good value, however, and I promised to return.

Kayseri was an exciting city to wander in except for the carpet touts. On one occasion I was accosted five times along a stretch of no more than 500 metres (about 500 yards) of the main road which runs beside the fortifications. I resisted the blandishments firmly but their persistence was an irritation. Once as I took a photograph a young man fell in beside me and started asking questions to which I gave no reply until I had completed my photography. He got quite angry and demanded to know why I would not answer. I told him I wished to concentrate. 'Are you free to talk now? I like speaking with strangers,' he said.

'Yes of course,' I replied, 'what do you wish to talk about?'

'You like Turkey?' he began, but carpets were what he had at the back of his mind.

'Yes,' I said, 'but I am not interested in carpets.'

'What do you mean?' He became still more angry because he had wasted his time, but once I had made plain that I was not a potential customer he disappeared. It was hard work.

My eye became bloodshot again, the result of reading the small print of my maps or the dictionary in the totally inadequate light of village houses or small hotels, so I bought a magnifying glass. Then I found a tiny, dimly-lit drinking place which I enjoyed as much for the custom as the beer. That place did a thriving business and for half an hour by my watch the big burly barman never paused in drawing beer – and this was only at five o'clock in the afternoon – while the waiters vied with each other as to how many full glasses they could carry at a time. I also found a second-floor balcony restaurant with a view southwards over a small mosque to the massive ridge leading up to Mount Erciyes.

Kayseri had the best muezzin callers I had yet heard. They competed across the city, striking up one after the other, demonstrating fine shades in the art of ululating, holding on until it seemed impossible that the high note could be sustained any longer and then, as one by one they finished and comparative calm descended over the city, one last defiant call would come from an unexpected corner, an extra long ululation from the champion caller of them all, determined to have the last word. I came across the Great Mosque: squat and low, of unusual architecture and indeterminate medieval date, it proved to be a gem inside with a fortune in rugs covering its huge expanse of floor. That evening I succumbed to a bad bout of diarrhoea.

The next morning I found I was passing blood with my diarrhoea which worried me but I had a busy schedule ahead and took a pill. I had decided to visit and climb Erciyes. I have always enjoyed climbing mountains, something I have only ever done on my own, and though I have never undertaken any serious rock-climbing I have from time to time found myself stuck in fairly perilous places. (It is always easier to go up than to come down, a rule that anyone who has done any climbing learns early, but one that I had often ignored until becoming stuck – or at any rate in danger of becoming so.)

I took a small red local bus the 11 kilometres (7 miles) to the village of Hisarcik. The bus was full of strong peasant women, each carrying one or more huge bundles, arguing good-humouredly with one another and all, apparently, organised by an old, thin-faced matriarch at the front. Hisarcik looked both pretty and prosperous. There was a further 15 kilometres (9 miles) from the village to the hotel where the winter skiers and the summer mountaineers stay. I walked out of Hisarcik, rising sharply, for it was already in the foothills of the mountain, and with my pack on my back I felt like the Pied Piper of Hamelin for I appeared to be followed by every small child in the village, calling, '*What is your name?*' or, alternately, saying 'My name is . . .'. The smallest boy of all ran at my side crying '*Baksheesh*'. Only at the edge of the village with the aid of a teenage girl who appeared from the last cottage and confirmed that I was on the correct road for Erciyes did I finally shake off this noisy entourage.

The road was cobbled and rose dramatically to reveal spreading out behind me the plain on which the city of Kayseri lies. I saw no dogs but kept a sharp look-out, ready for trouble. The going was slow, yet every few yards the vista below me would change and expand. Then a huge track came crawling up the road behind me; for a time I could hear and sometimes see it as it twisted and turned up the hillside. When eventually it came abreast of me at little more than walking speed the driver signalled for me to get in; there were two other men with him. He did not stop and I clambered aboard the moving giant to be greeted warmly with the usual offer of cigarettes. None of the men had any German and so conversation was limited.

The landscape was rocky and increasingly bleak yet surprisingly full of life. The purple, pink and white of small mountain flowers mingled everywhere with grey rock and dry brown earth. Busy in and out of the rocks were small stoat-like creatures which raised themselves up on their hind legs to peer in search of mates or enemies before scuttling off into the rocks again. As we rose still higher we passed long rows of beehives with pots of honey and honeycombs at the roadside to tempt passers-by. The beekeepers and their families had their tents set out on the hillside: they move the hives to the mountains in the height of summer to allow the bees to collect the honey from the mountain flowers.

We came to a complex of several large half-built hotels. The tourist industry had decided to expand the facilities at the base of the ski-run. The small hotel-hostel for skiers had been there for years but this was now being enlarged, and in addition two other much larger buildings, both apparently hotels, had just gone up: one appeared to be completed, the other was being built and there were several dozen workmen scrambling about the huge Swiss-style chalet with its steep pointed roof and overhanging eaves. The trucks which had given me a lift had brought building materials and the driver gestured towards the building where men were working and said something which I did not understand. I headed for the largest, most finished-looking of the three buildings. One door was locked, the whole seemed quite deserted, and yet clearly it was a hotel. At its other end I found a door which was open and entered; an elderly man looked at me in surprise. I asked if I could leave my pack there – by then it was twelve o'clock – as I wanted to head up the mountain ridge straight away. He shrugged his assent, so I filled my water-bottle with fresh cold water and set off.

I rose steadily past the first and then the second ski-lift huts. The hotel was at Dag Evi, which was already at 2,150 metres (7,050 feet). The peak of Erciyes is 3,917 metres (12,850 feet); a long ridge leads up to this and, about three-quarters of the way along it, is Red Rock, which rises sheer and presents real climbing problems. A second ridge runs down from the peak to the north so as to create a crater-like basin between the two ridges. From the top ski-lift it is possible either to head straight up the main ridge or to follow a path into the central crater. I give this detailed information because of what was to follow.

The top ski-lift is at a height of 2,774 metres (9,100 feet) so that by the time I had reached it from the hotel complex I had already climbed 624 metres (2,050 feet). That afternoon I began to discover the limitations of age; by the time I reached the ski hut I was exhausted. It was partly the unaccustomed height but apart from that I was simply not in training for such a steep climb, despite all the walking I had been doing. It was humiliating. I had to rest for 40 minutes at the ski hut because I was so exhausted; then I took the low path up into the crater between the two ridges. I trudged. Obstinacy came to my aid, and something of a second wind. High up in this crater-like valley I came upon the astonishing spectacle of huge blue and red plastic bowls full of water set out among the rocks. I had not seen a soul and for a while I could not imagine why they were there or who would want to leave them. Then a bee droned past me and I remembered the beehives. Bees will fly for miles to obtain water and, though there was dirty snow streaking the mountain, most of the year's melting was over and I had not come upon any water all afternoon. Drawn by these bowls of water the bees would then collect the honey from the wild flowers.

I forced myself slowly up the sides of the northern ridge and then followed that back to the ski hut. I was out of training, I was 55 and mountains make you learn about yourself: I had to admit that I was beginning to be past certain activities which I had always taken for granted. Two German youths were settling into the least exposed corner of the ski hut, and we talked a while. They said the hotel, at TL 4,000 was too expensive for them so they would camp there for the night. I told them they would freeze and then headed down the mountain. A large flock of sheep was meandering all over the approach to the hotels and I searched their ranks carefully for dogs: none were apparent.

Back in the curiously deserted hotel I found the caretaker, if that was his job, eating his supper. I did not want to disturb him but he insisted that I shared a great plate of rice, stew and tomatoes. I had a loaf of bread and some olives in my pack but when I went to get them in the hope of adding the olives to the meal as a relish he became angry, as though I was suggesting payment for his hospitality. After we had finished eating I asked about beds and then, finally, discovered that I was not in the hotel at all. He laughed with delight at my mistake, took me to the door and indicated the second of the buildings where most of the activity had been earlier in the day. The original hostel now nestled beneath a far larger addition. I shook hands with the friendly caretaker and walked the 200 metres to the hotel.

This was shut, but I found four men in a little back room. They instantly pressed tea upon me, assuring me that the hotel porter would come soon, and asking what I was doing. When I said I was climbing the mountain they asked my age. I must say references to my age were beginning to get me down, but when I said 55 they showed courteous amazement which mollified me. The hotel was more of a hostel, with eight bunk beds to a room, but I had a room to myself anyway: it reminded me of the Kingshouse Hotel in Glencoe. I had a large glass of tea and then retired to bed. My limbs ached with tiredness but I could not sleep. In any case I was up half the night with worsening diarrhoea, and passed more blood. I became seriously worried and tentatively diagnosed myself as having amoebic dysentery. This was of some comfort since I decided that my poor performance on the mountain that day was due to the debilitation of the disease rather than failing powers.

I was off up the mountain again the next morning shortly after six-thirty, this time with the whole day at my disposal. The first part was the worst and by the time I tackled the ridge I had got my second wind. In the early afternoon I met the two German boys coming down.

They had not got past the Red Rock, they told me, and they had almost frozen in the night. They filled my half-empty water-bottle from theirs since they were on the way down, having had the advantage of starting from the ski-lift three hours ahead of me. Once they had gone I enjoyed the loneliness of the mountain: the stillness and solitude to be found in such a place are rare gifts. Yet wagtails flitted past me continually, while circling far below in the crater where I had walked the day before I saw a pair of eagles whose harsh cries came clear through the thin air.

I knew when I reached it that I could not attempt the Red Rock on my own; in any case it was too late in the day and I was too tired. The ridge itself was the highest I have ever been. As I returned a sharp wind blew; to the south I could see Lake Yay-Golu and beyond in the misty distance the Taurus mountains. I got back to the hotel by seven o'clock and as soon as I had washed I went to the lounge, where the porter brought me a large glass of tea. I was immensely thirsty and when that was finished he at once brought me a second glass. Half-way through that I had to leave in a hurry for it brought on a fit of vomiting. Three Turks were sitting in a corner and the porter was also dancing attendance upon them. They asked me to join them for a glass of *raqi*, and turned out to include the president and director of the hotel complex. We spoke French. They were amazed that I had been up the mountain and they too inquired, politely, as to my age.

I had a wretched night of diarrhoea and passed more blood. The next morning I got a lift back to Kayseri with one of the foremen of the works and returned to the Camlica Hotel where I had stayed before and had left most of my gear. I put myself on a soothing diet of hot milk in the hope that it would deal with my diarrhoea and blood; of course it did nothing of the sort. I would have to seek medical advice.

# 21

# A Turkish Hospital

Hot milk is pleasant enough: drinking it relaxed the mind but did not solve the problem. I asked the hotel proprietor about doctors but he said they could be expensive and insisted that I should go to the hospital, so I walked there immediately after breakfast. It was a Sunday and most places were closed. The large hospital seemed totally deserted when I entered the forecourt – like the grave, I thought, a comparison which did not appeal to me! – but round the back I found an out-patients' entrance. The attendant, who spoke only Turkish, led me along a corridor to a small room occupied by a hospital policeman. He gave me a pad and pencil and I wrote: 'English – Doctor'. He nodded, gave instructions and the attendant took me to a young doctor who spoke English.

He was a charming man, that doctor. I described my symptoms, which was simple enough to do, and he translated into Turkish for the benefit of the nurse who was with us. Then he asked me to go with her and she took details which consisted solely of my name, address and age. The doctor arrived – we were in an open examination room with a dozen other people waiting for attention – so we were screened off behind green curtains while he examined me. 'You need a drip,' he said, 'but you do not need to worry.' I went with the nurse to a small empty ward with six beds, and lay on one of these for two hours with the drip attached to my left arm while I engaged in a sort of introspection induced by the possibility that I might have developed something unpleasant. The nurse looked in from time to time to adjust the rate of flow of my drip and then, when it was almost finished, the doctor arrived.

'How do you feel?' he inquired.

'Fine thank you, doctor.' I waited. He smiled the knowing smile common to doctors, whose power is greatest just before they impart information.

'You do not have amoebic dysentery', he paused, 'or cholera or typhoid or' – and he paused again, delicately – 'other things.'

I raised a quizzical eyebrow: 'What do I have, then?'

'*Castro*-enteritis', he said. He gave the first part of the name the unmistakable pronunciation of the Cuban leader but whether this was due to an inability to distinguish between English 'c' and 'g' or was the product of a right-wing sense of humour I was not to know. I experienced a sensation of enormous relief. He wrote out a prescription – two sets of pills and a liquid medicine which I had to take daily until they were finished – and told me where I would find a chemist which was open on Sunday. I asked how much I had to pay the hospital and he said nothing at all. So we shook hands and I left with that feeling which comes when a burden has been lifted, only then realising how much I had been worrying. The prospect of an unpleasant disease of the bowels holding me up in Turkey had not been an appealing one. The medicine cost me the equivalent of 3 pounds sterling and within a day the trouble began to clear.

Dogs and diarrhoea were the only two problems I had encountered in Turkey so far. In celebration of the happy outcome of my hospital visit I went to the *Bedesten* that afternoon to bargain for some kilims. I met my smooth salesman coming out of the Great Mosque with his family. He looked surprised at the sight of me for it was three days since last we had talked, before I went to Mount Erciyes, and he must have believed that I had gone for good. He was even more surprised when I said I would come to the shop in half an hour.

That setting was designed for a Hollywood spy thriller. The ancient caravanserai or *Bedesten* is situated at one corner of the large covered bazaar. The approach is through a small covered yard which then opens on to the square courtyard of the *Bedesten*. This has arches round it like a cloister; under each of these some different business is conducted. The carpet shops were on the upper level at the back of a covered balcony which also ran right round the courtyard and was approached by an outside flight of steps. Carpets hung over the balustrade to add colour to the dark grey-black of the stonework. I went up to find my flash friend waiting for me. The shop was perhaps 3.5 by 3.5 metres (12 by 12 feet), certainly no more. It was rich in rugs: they hung round the walls, they were stacked tight in corners, and the floor itself was triple covered with them.

I settled down for a lengthy session of bargaining. As a rule I maintain that bargaining is vulgar: if the price is too high, reject it and go elsewhere. Many years before I had gone into a shop in Tehran with a friend to buy some Persian miniatures and, when I had found what I wanted, paid the price demanded without demur. Outside, my friend berated me for not bargaining: he could have reduced the price by a quarter for me, he insisted. In fact bargaining can be great fun, and once I got into the mood I enjoyed myself.

The salesman suggested how we should proceed: he would show me rugs without naming a price and those I liked he put to one side. Then when there were enough set aside we could discuss their merits and decide upon prices. He piled the rugs before me, one on top of another, inviting me to feel the texture, giving little lectures about the methods by which they had been made: 'Pure wool, woven by hand. This is the area, the sheep for this wool are in the hills all round us.'

'Ah, the dogs', I murmured. Gradually the pile of selected rugs to the side grew until I felt there were enough from which to make my final choices, so the others were packed away by an attendant boy and a glass of lemon tea was brought for my refreshment.

Then the big man came in. The self-assurance of my salesman became as nothing in the presence of his boss, who treated him as though he were little more important than the boy who was stacking the unwanted rugs back in their corners. The boss was physically very large, with one of the biggest heads and widest mouths I have ever seen. He sported a day's growth of beard, turning salty grey, and had enormous hands. He exuded an easy worldliness ('we two could always do business together.') which appealed directly to me over the money-conscious efforts of the salesman. This time he had only come to check on progress and when he had been assured that I appeared to be a serious customer he departed again. He spoke English, German, French. 'More tea?' he asked as he left and at my nod barked an order to the boy, who disappeared smartly, to return almost at once with another glass for me. I presume they had a special samovar brewing round the corner for his customers.

Together we considered the individual merits of each rug that had been set aside and now my friend told me the price. I would react with horror: 'Beyond my pocket', I would say with a dismissive shrug. By the time I had waved aside seven or eight in this fashion the salesman was seriously worried.

'How much can you afford?' he asked, but to that question I gave no answer, kneeling instead to feel the texture of another rug. It was a game and I had just about perfected the art of showing indifference to his wiles when we came to the two rugs I really wanted. He haggled and settled on a price. He then wished to add an exorbitant sum to cover transportation to England, but finally agreed to half the amount. Now the boss returned.

He admired my choices and asked how long I had been in the country. We discussed dogs. 'They are all over these hills', he assured me, and went on to recount the story of a young German who had been badly bitten and had been obliged to spend the rest of his holiday money having anti-rabies injections. There was a jovial air of calculation about the boss. The salesman stood by nervously for although he had made a good sale to me he was afraid that at the last moment I might cancel, for so his mind worked, and as yet no money had changed hands. Not so the boss: he proceeded to ask me about Argentinians – 'what sort of men were they?' 'Macho', I replied. He laughed at that and told me another story: a young French couple had come in, but while she kept saying that they had to go to Erciyes he said he wanted to buy rugs.

'I said to the young man, do not have a fuss, come back to look at my rugs later, but the young man who had denied that he was French – "I am Argentinian" – said, "Now I buy carpets, she wait", and he took four hours looking through my wares while she was outside, there', and he gestured with one of his huge hands towards the balcony and gave a coarse chuckle of delight. 'Finally when it was dark that young man said "now we can go to Erciyes". She was silent when they went but that way she will be good in bed.' He laughed again. 'He was like us Turks, make them obey.' He told me this story while he rummaged round to find the correct papers and wrote out by hand a receipt for my Access card: 'I have no machine after four years though I keep asking them in Istanbul to send me one.' It was a performance and no doubt he produced others, varying them according to his estimate of the customer he wished to impress with his worldliness.

I paid in a mixture of travellers' cheques, credit card and ready cash and while we sorted this out the boss sent for two glasses of *raqi*. The rugs were packed in front of my eyes and addressed to my London flat. The salesmen were happy and I was satisfied, so we both enjoyed the *raqi*. The kilims were the only things I wanted to purchase on the trip and these were exceptionally fine examples. Now, having climbed the mountain, dealt with my sickness and purchased my rugs, I was ready to leave Kayseri.

# 22

# The Mayor of Koşçu

The road from Kayseri to Sivas runs west-north-west through a broad valley and for most of the distance (about 170 kilometres (105 miles)) its course is parallel to the Kizil Irmak, but road and river are separated by a line of hills. I wanted to visit places along the road, so that I would have to cross back and forth between river and road, although when I left Kayseri I headed north towards the hills and the little town of Erkilet.

Kayseri to Erkilet was an easy walk, a mere 11 kilometres (7 miles), most of it over flat farmland. At one stage I fixed my eyes upon a distant flock of sheep near the roadside, and only as I got nearer did they turn into a cluster of white-brown rocks without an attendant dog. Then I began a sharp upward incline to Erkilet, past some modern blocks of flats which were probably designed to relieve pressure on Kayseri.

Some people in the Camlica Hotel had assured me there was nothing to see in Erkilet. They were wrong. I suppose they had assumed that like most tourists I wanted certain minimal things – buildings to visit and a hotel to stay in, for example – and in that at least they did have a point. I toiled up a very steep hill into the little town and was examined with considerable interest by some men who inspected my backpack and walking-stick rather as though these were weapons of war.

Some of the old houses up the steep hill were set into the rock face. The view behind me to the plain of Kayseri was stunning, with Erciyes shrouded in a heat haze in the far distance. A group of men who sat drinking tea outside a house hailed me and we exchanged greetings. 'Was there a *lokanta*?' I asked, but no, there was no *lokanta*. 'A hotel?' No, there was no hotel either. 'Any place where I could get a meal?' They consulted, then one of the younger men told me to follow him and led me about 100 metres up the hill to a tiny village store where he explained my needs to the proprietor and a friend who spoke a little German. In fact his German was minimal but he claimed the ability to speak it so as to cast himself in the role of interpreter. This was unusual, for as a rule no excuse was ever deemed necessary to justify any amount of onlookers. The proprietor of the shop swept his arm across the top of a dirty table – I think it was the remains of an ancient butcher's chopping block – found a stool, and invited me to sit. He produced fresh bread, goat's cheese, tomatoes and a cold Fanta for me to drink. Later he sent a boy to bring tea. By that stage of my journey an 11-kilometre (7-mile) walk was nothing to me and in any case I was feeling especially buoyant because of the outcome of my hospital visit of the day before, but my appetite was always good and I tucked into the simple food with a pleasure which delighted my small audience. Others dropped in to inspect me, have a word with the shopkeeper and then go about their business. Once I had finished eating the questioning began, but the courteous way in which I was left to eat in peace ensured my ready response to the all-important interrogation which was to follow.

When they realised I was heading for the Kizil Irmak they became quite vehement in their claims that there was no road. 'You cannot go that way, it is many kilometres and there is no proper road', was the gist of their refrain. I produced my map and pointed to marks indicating tracks but they shook their heads. A bus stopped outside the shop and they suggested I took it.

'Where does it go?'

'Kayseri', they said.

'But I have just come from Kayseri.'

'But you cannot go over the hill; there is no way for you there.' The bus went and we continued a discussion which was getting me nowhere. Why they were so vehement in their attempts to persuade me not to continue on my way I never learned. In the end I took a photograph of the proprietor and a crippled boy – I think it was his son – and set off walking up the hill. The road rose sharply up the escarpment, which seemed set to go on for ever, and I was soon reduced to a slow measured plod. Then I heard the powerful notes of a tractor and before long one appeared labouring up the hill behind me, pulling a large trailer with high sides. The driver indicated his interest and drew in beside me; he pointed to the right-hand mudguard seat, the other being occupied by a boy of about 16, and I mounted. We tried out languages but neither of them spoke anything except Turkish, so that communication was limited. For most of our acquaintance we relied heavily upon sign language.

Over the top of the escarpment the road stretched into the distance across a rolling plain, but my tractor driver turned into a dirt track at right angles to the road and inquired by sign language whether I wished to come that way. Why not, I thought, so I nodded my agreement, willing to see where I should end up. We travelled a short distance towards an immense tumulus. Both driver and boy answered to the name Mustafa and now Mustafa senior pointed to the top of the tumulus: 'Hittit', he said, and asked whether I should like to visit it. I assented, and we drove up a track which circled the artificial mound to the top, where the massive stone remains of what I judged might have been a look-out tower offered a view for miles in every direction. The three of us wandered round the ruin; I took a picture of the two Mustafas, and then we descended to begin a memorable journey across the undulating countryside.

Mustafa maintained a spanking pace on his tractor and we drove for miles between huge wheat-fields, bean-fields, open grazing land and then more wheat-fields. We picked some raw chick-peas, which we ate as the tractor bounced along the dirt track, or we tried to light ciga-rettes. Mustafa waved greetings to groups of women in the fields and once we caught up with a huge flock of sheep whose great guardian shepherd dog turned to face us until the tractor almost ran him down.

It is difficult to judge distance on a tractor, especially when it is travelling fast, because the wind it creates gives the illusion of greater speed than is probably the case, but I reckon we had covered about 15 to 20 kilometres (9 to 12 miles) across this high plain of wheatfields when Mustafa turned off the track. We crossed several fields until we reached a tarpaulin covering a mound of harvested wheat, where we had a feast of fresh bread and melons. Mustafa senior now wandered off to call loudly across the fields while Mustafa junior let down the tailgate and began to shovel the wheat into the trailer.

Mustafa's long session of shouting was rewarded with the appear-ance of a shepherd boy on a donkey. He came up from a depression in the great field giving strange cries while he banged his heels into the donkey's flanks and waved a stick which he periodically cracked across its hindquarters. He was a brown-faced, wild-looking boy of about 17 with the curved beak nose of a gypsy and dark brown hair that stood up as if in perpetual surprise. He shook hands and then tackled half a melon while the elder Mustafa now called vigorously in the other direction towards a great flock of sheep that was crossing a hillside about 1 kilometre (half a mile) away. The sheep continued slowly out of sight round the spur of the hill, presumably under the control of dogs, while a lank youth of perhaps 18 came to greet us. He was a bit simple and merely stared uncomprehendingly at me. We loaded the wheat into the trailer, or rather the others did, for they refused to let me help. They did ask me, however, if I should like to ride the donkey – for their gratification, not mine – and I did so, or at least I sat astride it, kicked its ribs, whacked its rump and urged it to move in other ways. It was not very responsive and Mustafa asked to take a photograph of my efforts. I set the camera for him and he did so. Everything was crystal clear in the bright air.

At last we were loaded up: the boy with the donkey mounted and rode off, the lank simple youth strode away without a backward glance towards the hill round which his sheep had disappeared and we drove back to the path to continue on our way. After about 5 or 6 kilometres (3 or 4 miles) we began a steep, spectacular descent into a deep valley; it was richly green while a line of trees in the distance marked the banks of a river which turned out to be the Kizil Irmak. We came to a village overlooked by a ridge of rock caves. Mustafa stopped the tractor and pointed to these, suggesting a visit, so we walked up the steep hill to inspect a series of caves in a line along the escarpment like a village street. They were as interesting as anything I had seen in Cappadocia.

One cave had two huge logs in the form of a vice, the open end towards the cave mouth; here two uprights of equal massiveness supported a high crossbeam. A third upright log had been worked into the equivalent of a gigantic corkscrew which, when twisted, would – as far as I could work out – force the logs forming the vice upwards or apart. I tried in vain to discover what this had been invented to do. In a second cave was a huge millstone with attachments for an ox to turn it. After inspecting these and other caves we continued downhill into the village, where Mustafa delivered the trailer full of wheat to an old man. They had a long discussion of which I was the subject, for by then I was beginning to realise that Mustafa did not know what to do with me. The old man had no helpful suggestions to make either so Mustafa signed that I should mount the tractor again and we continued to the next village of Kosçu.

Here we stopped in the middle of the street and while I was being greeted by various passing old men I became a passive spectator to a problem of etiquette. Although by then my Turkish could still only be described as sparse I did have sufficient to follow the gist of a conversation even if I could not actively participate. The older Mustafa was saying: 'We can leave him here; we have given him a lift; we cannot be expected to do more.'

But the younger Mustafa was arguing: 'We cannot do that, we must at least help him find somewhere to stay for the night.' They battled round this problem and the younger Mustafa prevailed. The words 'town hall' and 'mayor' were used several times and that eventually proved to be the solution. The younger Mustafa signalled to me to get on the tractor once more. He reversed it and started off at such speed that I was thrown off, but once I had been retrieved we zoomed up the hill to the small town hall, outside which a group of men sat talking and eating. Mustafa explained my plight to them, much to their general amusement, so they promptly produced cheese, bread and tomatoes and tea for me. 'The mayor will fix it', I was assured by one.

Then a smooth young man with good English who had asked a question from an upper window came down to take charge of proceedings, which, of course, meant that he cross-examined me. 'Where have you come from? Where are you going? There is no hotel here. You cannot stop here', he said with authority, but by then it was already six o'clock and I had no intention of moving on. He produced a press card and explained his job: he was a student from Ankara and a number of them were spending the summer travelling to the small villages and towns to interview the mayors about their jobs. Having explained his presence and the fact that he had a car and would return to Kayseri that evening, he repeated that I could not stop in Kosçu; Turks, I sometimes thought, could become quite overbearing. I decided that I was going to stay in Kosçu and told him so. One of the other men who spoke French and to whom I had relayed this decision laughed good-humouredly and said I was quite right, the mayor would settle everything.

We sent upstairs into a smart office and my problem was explained to a man behind a big desk whom I took to be the mayor. Everybody crowded in to listen and there was much headshaking and laughter. Then the smooth young man was told that the mayor was now ready to see him in an inner room, so this was not the mayor at all. I was invited to sit in on his interview. We entered a well-appointed office with flags and group photographs on the wall where the mayor sat behind a larger desk than the one in the outside room. He rose to greet us, my presence was explained to him, we shook hands, he said he spoke German and had spent three years in Frankfurt, and then everybody settled down while the young man conducted his interview. I was given an easy chair to the side and three men sat round an occasional table which had a large silver tray of chocolates upon it. They helped themselves to these and one took a great handful of the chocolates and passed them to me, signalling that I should put them into my bag, which I did.

Meanwhile the young man took out a tape-recorder, set it up on the desk before the mayor and proceeded to ask his questions. He was less assured in this formal situation than he had been with me outside, while the mayor, a middle-aged, soft-spoken man who had seemed shy when he spoke to me, now took on great assurance and at every question held forth at didactic length. We spectators ate his chocolates.

Ahmet Kormaz was the mayor. He had greyish brown hair, a small neat moustache and a lined face with sagging cheeks which combined to make him look dour and depressed until he smiled, when his whole face lit up with friendliness. When the interview came to an end and the smooth young man said something about me he waved his hand in dismissal. So the smoothie with his French-speaking side-kick departed – not without provoking amused smiles from the older men – and then the mayor signalled to everyone to leave, and after locking up the mayoral office invited me to follow him.

I had thought they would find a corner for me in the town hall; instead Ahmet took me to his home. He had a fine house, on several levels, and showed me into his best sitting-room; wide wood platforms round three walls of the room were covered with cushions to form divans. We sat down to smoke while I discovered that despite three years in Frankfurt his German was very limited, though not as limited as my Turkish. He had four children: two boys of 21 and 20 who joined us, another of 22 who was away at the university and a daughter of 16.

Conversation was slow and I was tired: 30 kilometres (18 miles) bumping on the back of a fast-moving tractor can be as tiring as walking the same distance. Moreover, it caused aches in unusual places. Then a magnificent meal was served: soup followed by stew, rice, roast meat and vegetables. The mayor and his two sons ate with me; the women of the household never appeared. When the boys had cleared the food away coffee and plums were brought. We attempted more conversation but by then it was past nine o'clock and the mayor was clearly as tired as I, so by mutual consent we wished one another good night, and he produced bedding from a wall cupboard which we arranged on the wooden divan at one side of the room. He took me to see the toilet and then I retired to bed, although I had to mend my trousers first, for due to my carelessness while sitting on the tractor mud-guard they had been ripped by the huge wheel as I leant too far outwards. I fell asleep to the sound of the village dogs.

# 23

# The Road to Sivas

I awoke to peaceful silence to discover that Kosçu came alive quite late in the morning, at least in the mayor's house. It was not until eight o'clock that the mayor appeared, followed by trays of food for a magnificent breakfast which was laid out in the guest-room for us. Two of his friends joined us and, with the younger of his sons, we made a breakfast party of five. Talk came round to dogs – a number had been barking furiously in the night – and predictably everyone laughed at my concern. One of the guests spoke reasonable German and had spent longer than his friend the mayor in Germany, or at least had learnt the language better. The second visitor referred to him good-naturedly as 'the capitalist' and I gathered he had saved a good deal of money which now gave him considerable standing in the village.

When I was ready to depart I took a photograph of the mayor and his son standing on the roof of the kitchen, on to which we stepped from the best room which I had occupied during the night. Many village houses were constructed on more than one level, depending upon the nature of the ground: Kosçu occupied steep hillsides and part of a narrow valley which twisted down to the Kizil Irmak. The mayor's small black and white mongrel dog, which had wagged its tail at me in friendly fashion while I took the photograph, now ran in to bite my leg.

There was one more surprise to come. The mayor insisted that he would take me the 8 kilometres (5 miles) from the village to the Felahiye road. I protested that he must have other things to do but he was politely adamant. He had a truly battered old car of an indeterminate make which refused to start, but having committed himself he was not going to be defeated. I wandered up and down for about 20 minutes – I have no mechanical aptitude and deemed it useless to offer help or advice – while he alternately used an old crank handle and fiddled inside the bonnet. An eventual splutter brought the engine to life but by then the door on the passenger side was jammed open and another operation was required to shut it. We wound slowly through the dusty village and then by the river, which was small and beautiful between green tree-lined banks. In a second village we had to stand with the engine idling for ten minutes because the road was blocked by a tractor and large truck. I was fearful that if the engine stopped we should not be able to start it again but this did not happen and eventually we cleared that village to rise into open, treeless hill country. When we did reach the road where I was to begin walking again the mayor insisted upon thumbing down another car to give me a lift. His motives for this unwanted action were unclear but I think comprised a mixture of three things: in part a natural courtesy to help me on my way, for no more than anyone else did he believe that I wanted to walk; in part he was discharging his mayoral duty to someone who had been his (official) guest; and in part, I believe, he wished to make sure he got me clear of his parish which in this case meant him!

For some reason that stretch of the journey – Kosçu to Sivas – remains in my memory as a series of vignettes rather than a more rounded whole. It was magnificent walking country and 30 kilometres (18 miles) made a good day despite the continuing high temperatures but it was never that easy. I got lifts not only unsolicited by thrust upon me, again becoming aware of the 'German factor' in Turkey. I inspected a few ruins – a massive ancient caravanserai at Sultankhan or a crumbling tower in the middle of nowhere – and almost for the first time I looked upon one of the great dogs with a sense of appreciation.

At Gemirek, as I was walking along the main Sivas road, I stopped early in a small hotel that overlooked a busy garage. Here I sat on a balcony and wrote for four hours – at least I would have written for that length of time had I not been constantly diverted by the scene below me, where the long-distance buses drew in to disgorge their passengers for a 20 minute break before their drivers hooted and started off again on the minute. An old man, a caretaker from the nearby *lokanta*, peered up at my balcony from time to time and signed for me to come down and take tea with him. But I needed to be on my own and that balcony allowed me to be both public and private at the same time, a punishment to the curious Turks who so wanted to know what I was doing!

On another occasion I was deposited in the centre of a village square by a tractor whose driver had given me a lift for several kilometres. Two men who were passing the time of day at once turned to wave me imperiously to their sides: what was I doing; where was I from; why was I there? The catechism was exhaustive and thorough, but I was used to such demands by then and did not feel irritated. But when they had finished to their satisfaction they turned to one another again to continue their interrupted conversation: I was dismissed! This, indeed, was one of the more disconcerting ways in which conversations of inquiry – I called them inquisitions – could be terminated.

Once as I toiled up the road towards a pass where great rocks were scattered on the steep hillside I became conscious of the deep warning barks of a dog. For a time I did not see it and was not sure whether the barking was aimed at me or some other target. But then I saw him: a magnificent shepherd dog. He sat on the hillside like a lion with his paws out in front of him, the iron spiked collar round his neck, his head proudly raised as he barked from 50 metres up the hillside above, warning me to keep clear. I waved my stick as I kept on my way and the dog did not consider that it need move. On another occasion when I was in a crowded *dolmus* which had stopped so that driver and passengers alike could insist that I accepted a lift we rounded a hillside to be faced by five great dogs racing furiously at us, for their flock was just nearing the road. In the circumstances I was retrospectively glad that I had allowed myself to be persuaded to take the lift only 1 kilometre (half a mile) back along the road.

One early morning when I was enjoying the freshness of the day a big Volvo carrying Austrian plates stopped with a squeal of brakes just ahead of me to allow its driver to lean from the window to watch my approach. He insisted upon giving me a lift. His name was Mustafa Basel and he was an interesting example of someone much influenced by the 'German factor'. He had worked for years in Austria, he told me, and was just back on a visit. He only took me a few kilometres before turning into a village where he wanted to have his car cleaned, so that his lift made little difference to my journey, but that was hardly the point.

Mustafa took me off to a tea-house, leaving his car in line for a clean behind a great truck that was having something else done to it. Though he asked me the usual questions he was really far more concerned to tell me of his achievements in Austria. It turned out that he would return to Austria the next day with his family, who lived in that village, and the journey would take five days. He constantly fingered his bunch of keys, attached to which was a tiny silver abacus whose little balls he counted endlessly between thumb and forefinger, I think quite unconsciously. It was a sophisticated alternative to the prayer beads carried by most Turkish men – 'worry beads' would be a better description in many cases – and one that would pass inconspicuously in non-Turkish surroundings.

That village had a Roman foundation, he told me, although there was nothing Roman to see. We stood in the busy little street smoking while acquaintances came up to greet him and inquire about me: that, really, was why we stood there. I was often used as a sort of status symbol in this fashion by men who had worked abroad, usually in Germany, and wished to show that they could interpret me to the curious, which meant anyone else who happened to be around.

Mustafa was one of many who brought home to me the importance of the German factor in Turkey. The German relationship is the most important of Turkey's ties with the Europe of which she so much wants to be a part, and the connection is apparent in a number of ways. German is the second language of the country and as I was to find again and again I could get by with some German where no other language was understood. There were many cars with 'D' plates on them and at first I thought they belonged to German tourists, busy quartering the whole country. Only after a while did I realise that they belonged to Turks who had worked in Germany and had either returned with their German car for good or were on a home visit. The large numbers of Turks working in West Germany are a source of welcome remittances home, while those who return bring with them concrete evidence of their new prosperity: cars, radios, hi-fi and video sets being the most conspicuous examples. In many places such as Kosçu I met Turks who might have spent 15 years of their working lives in West Germany to return home rich in terms of their village, able to spread a measure of that wealth to both their families and the village as a whole.

But there was another side to the German connection: the boy in Nevşehir on the verge of a nervous breakdown; the inevitable complications that people who belong to two cultures have to face. I saw evidence of this when I was befriended by those who had been to Germany. Sometimes there was an edge of desperation, disguised as traditional Turkish hospitality, in their determination to help me. In reality they wanted to reassure themselves that they did belong to both worlds, of the traditional Turkey and the Germany where they had spent much of their working lives.

It was lovely walking weather, with the first hints of the coming autumn in the air. The railway from Istanbul ends at Sivas, the furthest point of the nineteenth-century dream of a Berlin to Baghdad line, and here it ran parallel to the Sivas road. From Sarkisla I walked back across the hills on the long bleak road to Akcakisla on the other side of the Kizil Irmak. In one *lokanta* which served beer I was able to get cold mutton for the first time. I often asked for it thereafter but found it only rarely.

At last I reached Sivas. This is an ancient town and was one of my landmarks, a place in which to pause because it marked the end of a section of the journey. There I could consider the next phase to be tackled while 'taking stock' – my euphemism for washing clothes.

# 24

# Sivas

I detected the first hints of autumn on the walk to Sivas although it remained hot: a slight wind blew a coolness across the land, a reminder of changes to come. The city lies on the Kizil Irmak, but here also the mountains retreat and the valley widens into a plain. Sivas, the Roman Sebasteia of the first century AD, is an exciting city. It achieved its greatest importance during the Seljuk sultanate of Rum and its most impressive mosques and other public buildings are all Seljuk and date from that time. Sivas has been a trading centre of importance since ancient times for it lies on the great caravan routes to Persia and Baghdad; the region is a rich grain and wool-producing area and also famous for its wines.

I intended to stay in Sivas for several days so picked a reasonable hotel at the princely sum of TL 6,000 a night. Then I set off to explore the town. Walking and the hot weather had combined to give me a more or less permanent thirst so that once I had settled anywhere my first priority was always to locate the *Fici Bira* sign, a shield with a tankard of beer upon it, denoting a drinking house or pub. Even big towns only had one or two such establishments; some of the smaller places where I stayed had none. I found two *Fici Biras* in Sivas though there may have been more.

There is a large modern square opposite the town hall but on the other side of that, behind a popular tea-garden in which the old men congregate, lie the remains of the ancient city: these are mainly thirteenth-century and ruins, but elegant none the less, monuments to a splendid if historically brief period of Turkish history. They include what is left of a Seljuk hospital, the *Cifte Minare* (a Koranic school) which is considered to be the most beautiful monument in Sivas, and a small, elegant mosque. I bought some long, carved cigarette-holders, persuading myself that they were presents but in fact desirous of smoking through them myself. Then I sat in the tea-garden to watch the world go by. By the time I reached Sivas I had become a tea-garden addict, and I would happily sit for hours in such places, periodically ordering a tea, but otherwise content to watch others go bustling, or ambling about their business. I would smoke through one of my collection of holders, naturally not inhaling since I was to abandon the practice of smoking as soon as I left Turkey, content to let time pass. Sometimes I would be approached by curious Turks, whom I always invited to sit a while with me if they so wished. On my own I spent the time in contemplation.

I weighed myself again to find I was still 5.4 kg (12 lb) lighter than when I left London, and felt trim and fit.

I went into the *Ulu Camii* or Great Mosque. Built in the twelfth century and famous for its eleven arcades of pillars, it is now a teaching mosque and all over its huge floor space boys sat at lecterns with open Korans from which they recited aloud, a high-pitched babble of rote-learning, the young voices rising up and down in a wave of crescendoes. What attracted me about Sivas was the fact that sandwiched between its many historic sites were crowded markets, busy shops and bustle. The fruit and vegetable market was one of the most colourful I had seen and I bought huge ripe peaches, plums and grapes at ridiculously cheap prices.

Nothing seems more dead than the history of the immediate past. I visited the Atatürk Museum, the former high school where the Congress of 1919 launched the revolution under the presidency of Mustafa Kamal (Atatürk). The school looks like a museum from the outside, while inside I had to search before an attendant appeared, startled at foreign custom, to show me round. Everything had been kept as it was in 1919, with the addition of period photographs. I also visited the *Inonu* Museum, which was the statesman's house and is still treated as though it were a private home so that on entry I had to take off my shoes. I did not realise this at the time so that the old lady who had opened up for me – it was firmly locked and clearly also lacking custom – was obliged to gasp in a suitably horror-struck manner while pointing to my feet, before I did so. Then she relaxed and showed me round.

There are two high points in Sivas and I visited both. On the outskirts of the town a modern mosque perches on a tall rock. I had to walk through an old part of town to approach this and discovered, as I often did, how quickly the acceptance of a stranger which was normal in the centre of any big town like Sivas became something quite different the moment I strayed from the beaten track. The section through which I now walked was clearly unfrequented by visitors even though it was no more than a few hundred metres from the main square. I was stared at, if not with incredulity at least with a degree of suspicion, women covered their faces at my approach along the small streets, and dogs barked threateningly – although for me this was to be expected, a kind of *de rigeur* response which I now demanded of all Turkish dogs. Several burials were in progress in the grounds of the cemetery and from that high point I looked down on the whole of Sivas and managed to locate most of its landmarks.

The other high point consisted of the long, coffin-like ridge of the Kali Park with tea and refreshment gardens at either end of it, one producing blaring music from loudspeakers, the other being arranged for live entertainment after dark. I enjoyed a large pot of tea, virtually my own samovar for a change, and watched a brilliant sunset colour the distant hills as I became conscious of a distinct evening chill in the air. Back in the hotel I found my room had been invaded by workmen, who were plastering a hole in the wall.

The Kizil Irmak at Sivas is a disappointment: it strives to be grander than a mountain stream but hardly succeeds as it meanders through the wide plain on which the city stands. And yet a short distance downstream from Sivas, back along the way of my approach, it is pretty, sparkling between tree-lined banks. One of the extraordinary aspects of the Kizil Irmak, the longest river in Turkey, is that for mile after mile it does not appear to change its size. It meanders in its bed, sometimes between steep cutaway banks, sometimes spread out with sandbanks rising to form islands between divided streams. Near Sivas, sadly, it appeared to be heavily polluted, the recipient of much of the city's sewerage. I was, however, seeing it at the height of the summer dry season and later it would have been swollen by the spring thaws of the mountain snows.

# 25

# Central Anatolia

Before continuing east along the Kizil Irmak I decided to make a trip back across the high centre of Anatolia from Sivas to Yozgat. This would take me very nearly across the middle of the region enclosed by the two rivers. I wanted to get the feel of the plateau and give my journey an extra dimension: the Americans would say that such a rounding-off trip would ensure that I gained a 'total experience'.

I decided to use public transport for this part of the journey. My first objective was the town of Yildizeli and since the railway from Sivas to Amasya passes through it I tried to travel by train, but unfortunately there was only one that night and I did not wish to travel in the dark. At the main bus station, diligent inquiry revealed that no buses would take me there either but a man who overhead my inquiries explained that I needed a local bus from the centre of town: he then insisted upon taking me back there in his empty *dolmus*.

The bus was one of the small red local ones which made a number of stops to cram in more passengers before we set off on the 40-kilometre (25 mile) ride. At first we followed the Kizil Irmak back down its valley, but before long we rose steeply into bleak hills where we turned off the road to visit a village of tents surrounding a solitary mosque. This was a resort famous for its hot springs to which families came, set up their tents, took the waters and then departed.

Yildizeli lies at the base of precipitous bleak hills. It was a dusty, dirty place in a confusion of huge holes since its streets were all ripped up into enormous trenches for the installation of new sewerage. There was nothing to see or to do in Yildizeli and strangers were very definitely regarded as strangers. Since it was also quite a small place I was immediately conspicuous and remained so for the length of my visit. As usual I began by wandering round the town simply to get my bearings; more than once I was asked what I wanted. It was, I think, assumed that I had got off the bus by mistake: I was not meant to be there. Certainly one man came up to tell me that the next bus for Yozgat – or 'did I want to go to Sivas?' – was not for another two hours. But no, I wished to stay in Yildizeli. 'What do you mean, stay in Yildizeli? What do you want to do here?' He was quite indignant!

I decided to walk the bleak range of hills above the town so I had an early lunch in one of the two *lokantas* on the main street and then checked into a tiny hotel at the back of a dirty courtyard. The proprietor took me through small dormitory bedrooms each with three or four beds to the one single room with key, the best. The bed, however, was occupied by a young man, I think part of the hotel staff. He was promptly ejected: the room was now mine and I could rest. The landlord seemed to think I was in immediate need of sleep. I left my things there – no clean sheets were offered – and set off for the hills.

A steep dirt road twisted and narrowed its way up towards the hills. A small, pretty mosque and pleasant, though unkempt, tea-garden lay to one side of the road, after which it rose even more sharply. Sewage was thrown into the street so that the middle of the narrow hill was a muddy slipway of water and refuse which forced me to take long steps from side to side as I sought dry ground. Women in purdah sat on doorsteps and eyed me carefully as I toiled upwards; those whose mouths were not already covered promptly pulled their headscarves across their lips at my approach. Children called out their invariable greeting: '*What is your name?*' and men looked at me with a certain belligerence: What was I doing there and why? Two raised their hands in the cupped gesture of inquiry which I had come to expect though they did not say anything. A third, however, came up to ask where I was going: 'There is nothing up here', he said. But I was ready for that, and pointed beyond the last houses to the bleak hills which appeared above them. That seemed to satisfy him: most Turkish men with whom I spoke appreciated hill walking. The majority in any case either were or had been shepherds at some stage in their lives.

More than most of the places I had visited, Yildizeli made me aware of how delicate is the line between welcome and hostility. It is very easy for the stranger to appear prying: what was I doing in Yildizeli? Why was I there? What business had I, a stranger from another, infinitely more prosperous country, to be walking through its small poor streets where people lived out half their lives on their doorsteps? Only when I told the man I was off to walk the hills did his belligerence relent, to be replaced by a partial understanding. Had I replied instead that I was just looking at the town I might have received a very different response.

Such reflections brought me back to the subject of curiosity. I am personally always indignant at the prying of others: my business is my own, yet as a traveller I am profoundly curious. The justification for this, I tell myself, is a kind of scientific inquiry, the need to know, so that later I can interpret to others. Thus, I am only being curious in the abstract – in this case about the people of Turkey generally – rather than about individuals. Yet it is very easy for such curiosity to be mistaken for prying into poverty. The line of differentiation between abstract and personal inquiry can wear pretty thin and, of course, though in my case such a line did really exist, the reverse, to which I could hardly object, was the ceaseless inquiry to which, as an individual, I was constantly subjected throughout my journey.

At the top of the narrowing dirt road I passed between two houses to find myself half-way up a gully with nothing but the hills rising beyond. When I got up higher I could see how Yildizeli spread up several gullies as though the town was a splayed hand, its fingers reaching towards the hills. The day was unbelievably clear, the sun sharp, the sky without any clouds so that the hills were outlined in brilliant relief. I rose steadily for 300 metres (1,000 feet) over close-cropped, short-tufted grass. It was clearly sheep country and as I realised this I also realised that for once I had left my walking-stick behind. From then onwards I kept an especially sharp look-out for sheep and their attendant guard dogs, ready for war with the latter at any moment.

The weather was perfect for walking and I walked for miles along the stark hills, the broad plain spread out below me, one road cutting across it westwards towards Yozgat, another striking out north, straight as an arrow, to Tokat and Amasya. When I topped the ridge a breeze which sometimes developed into a wind kept me cool though I got sunburnt for I had also forgotten to bring my hat.

On hills I always contemplate. By then I was about half-way on my journey, and sitting on a rock on that lonely windswept Turkish hillside I reviewed a moderately useless life. I decided that of all things I had done most could just as easily have been done by someone else or indeed have been left undone. I felt that I had managed not to disturb too many people, but, reflecting upon a life which in worldly terms had hardly produced very much, I found that I did not mind.

When I returned to the town in late afternoon I spent an hour in the tea-garden by the mosque. It was time for prayers and a succession of old men came along the path to the mosque. Later, as part of a popular and hallowed ritual, they sat in the tea-garden to meet their friends and gossip. Various of them came over to greet me and one or more sat for a while talking, calling for more tea, insisting I was their guest. Then they would return to their own group and pass on what they had learned about me. A small boy came to greet one of the men, who told me with great pride that he was his sixth son. Turks make a profession of having big families and glory in being prolific. Once, when discussing Turkey's application to join the European Community, we got on to the subject of population. I have a precise head for figures and when the question cropped up said that I thought Turkey had a population of fifty-one million.

'What is the population of Britain?' I was asked.

'Fifty-six million', I replied.

My questioner smiled indulgently: 'Turkey', he said, 'now has sixty million people.'

Spontaneous hospitality and kindness mixed with a strong dose of determined curiosity is one of my abiding impressions of Turkey. That night, in the small entrance to my hotel, where reception, restaurant and drinking place combined, I drank *raqi* at my small table and periodically, as though I was holding court, invited the next curious person to be seated while he tried to find out all about me. In the morning I walked the 2 kilometres (1 mile) to the main road to catch the next bus to Akadagmeni. I spent an hour in the bus-stop tea-house drinking teas which were contributed by the curious, as men and youths came in succession to talk with me.

The country between Yildizeli and Akadagmeni began to change, and more green appeared. We crossed a wide valley, almost a plain, and then suddenly, as was always the case, the hills closed in upon us once more and we toiled up passes. Now there was some stunted forest although the vegetation consisted mainly of bushes rather than trees. The bus did not turn into Akadagmeni but left its passengers by the petrol station at the junction of the town road and the highway to Yozgat. I had hardly adjusted my pack when the garage owner hailed me: 'Tea?'

'Of course, why not?'

The owner's son, a bright boy of thirteen, took the money for petrol sales. He spoke good English and acted as our interpreter. 'What did I want to do in Akadagmeni?' 'See it.' But such an answer did not satisfy. 'There is nothing to see,' I would be told, but though this was not correct the things I wanted to see were difficult to explain. Modern tourism has a great deal to answer for.

I walked into Akadagmeni – which like Yildizeli had half its roads up, apparently also waiting for the installation of new drains – booked into a small hotel on a steep hillside, then set out to explore the town.

It was a bustling place. On a bluff overlooking the market square a new park had been laid out. Carefully selecting a lone seat which gave a fine view of activities below I lit a cigarette ready for a little contemplation before lunch but, of course, I was wasting my time. A group of teenage boys, two of whom wished to practise their high school English, drifted up to talk and find out where I came from. They were friendly, curious and fun, yet I would have liked to relax on my own. Turks, however, take for granted their right to approach and interrogate a stranger at will. I escaped them after a while and found an excellent *kebap salonu* where the host and a French-speaking friend insisted I joined them for tea when my meal was over.

We discussed Turkey's application to join the European Community, following from my comment upon the fact that the roads here, as in Yildizeli and other places, were all up for new drains. The explanation, I was told, was '*that Turkey was now mounting*'. The topic of Turkey's application to join Europe was a popular one and I was often called upon to explain why Turkey could not be admitted at once. I had three explanations: the first, opposition by Greece, which was accepted automatically; the second, opposition by the southern Catholic countries which, though they may not voice the fact openly, do not relish the idea of Muslim Turkey joining Christian Europe, which was also accepted, though as an obstacle to be overcome (Turkey, after all, is now a secular state). My third explanation, for me the crucial one, was simply that the main European countries do not wish their 'rich man's club' to be joined by so large and poor a country as Turkey since this would dilute the economic advantages and turn the community into something quite different from what it is and what was originally envisaged. Language difficulties made this a hard argument to get across but in the end I succeeded in doing so, to the moritifation of my French-speaking friend who, however, was compelled reluctantly to agree with me.

Only when I got up to go and the French-speaking Turk came to point the way to an old Byzantine church did I discover that he was lame. Earlier we had discussed the Armenians: there had once been a substantial minority of them living in the town but they had all gone, he told me. I did not inquire how or why, perhaps because at that moment I thought of Gladstone fulminating against Turkey at the end of the nineteenth century because of the 'Armenian massacres'.

I walked out of the town towards forested hills, making sure that I had my walking-stick with me, and missed the Byzantine church as I meandered through small lanes. I passed a long line of tractors and trailers full of wheat, their drivers idling in talk as they waited their turn to enter a great barn to offload. As I left the town behind, rising past a prosperous-looking farm, several women called out greeting to me and one who spoke good German asked where I was off to. This was certainly unusual, and a welcome change from inquiry only from men. Not often was I addressed like that by women.

The forest above the town was thick with great pine trees and stunted oaks. A cowherd on a donkey came past me on his way to his herd which I came to later, higher up. I walked along the bleak, exposed ridge and then returned across a valley thickly covered by forest. I had thought to be alone but three times met with men or boys herding cattle among the trees. On my way back to Akadagmeni, having described a circle in the hills, I came upon three boys sitting idly while their cows munched through the thick bush. Normally in such encounters the Turks would greet me first but on this occasion I called *merhaba* to them; they looked back solemnly in silence.

When I came back into the outskirts of the town the same group of women who had questioned me as I set out now hailed me from a garden, where they were eating under the shade of a great tree while small children shouted and played round them. They invited me to join them and eat. There was one older woman and three very pretty young ones, each wearing traditional headscarves fringed with beads. One of the younger women went into the house to return with fresh bread, goat's cheese and stewed red cherries. I wanted tea for my thirst more than anything else so they gave me several glasses and then I ate some of the food. They asked the usual set questions I expected on such occasions; what was unusual about this encounter was the complete absence of men and the readiness of a group of women to entertain a stranger – until this meeting I had only been entertained by women if their menfolk were also present. They made a charming group sitting on the grass, laughing and playing with the small children who constantly circled round us, and I wondered if I would be allowed to take a photograph. Eventually I asked the older woman whether she would object. She did, most strongly, with the emphatic negative *yok yok*. It was an interesting contrast: their readiness to have me join them as a guest and feed me, and the sudden drawing of the line at the suggestion of any photographs.

When I continued back through the town I was greeted by men in French, which was unusual. The tractors, lined up with their harvest of wheat, did not appear to have moved at all during my long afternoon of walking. In an obscure corner in the centre of town I found a pub, which was dark and at first sight appeared scruffy and uninviting. I had to sit on a high stool by a wallside ledge but after a short while the host, a bustling cheery man, came to serve me, apparently delighted at my appearance. A grim man sitting nearby continued to look grim but others showed friendly interest and before long the host invited me over to his table, where he was in conversation with a number of his cronies. Two spoke English and were teachers, one spoke French. A fourth big fellow told me he was a boxer and offered to box me but since he was bigger and 25 years younger, I declined that offer and we had another beer instead. The town was dark and very quiet when I left the pub though it was only just after eight o'clock. In my hotel a number of guests had materialised; they sat in the dim lounge glued to the television, so I went to bed.

# 26

# Yozgat

The next morning I took a *dolmus* to Yozgat; it proved to be one of the most uncomfortable drives I can remember. The driver insisted that I should take a seat in the front next to him and for a while I sat in comfort while the little bus filled up with passengers. Yozgat was evidently a popular place and the driver was determined upon a full load, yet no one else was invited to the front and I thought my luck was in. It was not. At the last moment or so it seemed, for a *dolmus* only departed at the whim of its driver, a huge man of Falstaffian proportions who dispensed loud comments and greetings without cease to all and sundry opened the front door as of right, to push me across to the centre by the gears and the driver. He occupied one and a half seats. At last, carrying more passengers than either safety or comfort dictated, we departed. Someone from behind thrust a great bundle of fresh green peas on a stalk into the hands of 'Falstaff', who promptly divided the present in two and gave me the smaller portion. 'Falstaff's commentaries to the other passengers, most of whom he appeared to know, continued remorselessly throughout our drive and this necessitated his turning round all the time, much to my increased discomfort. I podded the chick-peas and munched them.

Meanwhile the countryside changed perceptibly from wide open wheat land to more closed hills with scatterings of stunted forest. We stopped several times to pick up yet more passengers and when it really did seem that the bus could not hold another person the driver invited a man into the front. He sat wedged between me and 'Falstaff', most of his weight upon my right knee. When we stopped at a traffic police control point I thought they would protest at our overcrowded condition but nothing was said and we proceeded to Sorgun, 'Falstaff', whose sheer bulk meant no one could sit on his knee, talking more loudly to ensure that everyone in the crowded *dolmus* would hear him.

At Sorgun, the only place of any size on the way to Yozgat, we lost quite a few of our passengers including the one from my knee, and I began to relax. 'Falstaff' got out, but instinct warned me he would be back; meanwhile the driver offered his wares. *Dolmus* drivers shout their destinations at passers-by or, more generally, into the street at large, repeating the name of the town to which they are going several times over on a rising note, the final repeat drawn out in a kind of singsong: 'Yozgat, Yozgat, Yozga-a-a-at'. 'Falstaff' returned with a paper carton of ice-cream and two wooden scoops stuck into it. He invited me to partake with him, so there were compensations for my uncomfortable position after all.

Sorgun had a bustling main street where we had stopped to recruit passengers but otherwise looked uninteresting. That, however, was simply because I was not getting out. Contrary to many people who map out their journey between the places they deem to have interest for them I hate to pass even a small place by, since it might contain something worth visiting which I only hear of later or provide an unexpected encounter or adventure. Passing by, as I now did Sorgun, always left me with a feeling of loss: what might have happened had I stayed there?

Despite the ice-cream I was in a bad temper when finally we reached Yozgat and more than glad to see the back of 'Falstaff', who in any society would qualify as a prize bore. Yozgat is a large modern town less than 40 kilometres (25 miles) from Hattusas so that, by returning there from Sivas, I had described an elongated circle since leaving Sungurlu – and that already seemed a long time back in my travels.

Half the centre of Yozgat had been dug up to provide more huge trenches ready to receive drains – yet another indication that Turkey was '*mounting*'. I booked into the Saray Hotel but nothing was ready and the receptionist suggested that I should stay away until three in the afternoon, by which time I would be able to use my room. It was then eleven o'clock, so I left my pack at the desk. This did nothing to improve my temper. I then quartered the centre of town in search of a *Fici Bira* sign but none was to be found. Instead I found a *lokanta* which also served beer, something of a rarity, and ordered one, but the waiter was unwilling to serve me unless I ate as well. I became obstinate: 'I just wanted a beer', I said, and refused to budge. The waiter indicated that they were already full of early diners but I was not impressed. He went to consult the manager, who was carving from an enormous doner kebab. The manager was a man of discernment: he took one look at me and said, 'Give him a beer.'

My seat was by a low-lying window that looked out on huge ditches crossed by precarious plank bridges and piles of earth over which pedestrians had to scramble to reach the large square beyond. A nearby clock tower provided a central meeting place. A plaza in the middle of the square looked stark and bare but sloping upwards beyond that was a tea-garden well shaded by trees. My hotel – TL 3,000 a night – was off to the right. After I had drunk a second beer I began to relax: it had all been 'Falstaff's fault. Then I ordered a kebab lunch and the hovering waiter relaxed as well.

The day was exceptionally hot and when finally I got into my hotel room it was to find there was no water, either lukewarm or cold, so I could not take a shower. I wrote up my notes, rested for a while and then went out to the central tea-garden. It could have been lovely; the trees were fine and the site perfect but as with many other tea-gardens it managed to convey a sense of decay: broken paving stones, piles of rubble and corners of collected rubbish whose jaded appearance of permanence suggested a municipal plot to downgrade all tea-gardens. I drank tea and smoked while watching a succession of beggars do the rounds of the tables. Then I set off to explore the town, whose most impressive monument is an eighteenth-century mosque. Yozgat rises up the hills on either side of the valley and is neatly split in two by the main highway which I had travelled that morning: this continues to Ankara.

A national park lies about 7 kilometres (4 miles) to the south of Yozgat and I was heading for this up a steep hill through the outskirts of the town when I was hailed by a group of men drinking tea in a large open yard. Would I join them? It was a vehicle maintenance depot and they were mechanics. One spoke good German, and several of them had worked there for at least a few years. They gave me tea, inquired where I came from and much else of my business and lineage. Then I departed.

Turkish curiosity, as I discovered more than once, took odd forms. On this occasion, for example, the circle of eight men I joined – an original four who had promptly doubled at my arrival on the scene – all showed the greatest attention while I responded to the questions of their chief German interpreter, as though my appearance had made all the difference to their day, yet when I announced that I had to leave they accepted my decision without demur, turning at once to conversations of their own.

Shortly after leaving behind the last buildings I came to a gateway into the national park where I had to pay a TL 250-entrance fee. The road rose among increasingly thick-trunked, tall pine and fir-trees and

I began to enjoy the walk. But almost at once a car skidded to a stop beside me, and its three occupants, all men, invited me to take a lift up to the park hotel; though I really wanted to walk I accepted their offer. Refusing lifts had produced more than one heated exchange: 'What do you mean, you want to walk? No one walks! Come with me, I have a car, I will take you!' In my travelling mood, which embraced a readiness to accept things as they occurred, I found it easier to take the lifts which were offered than to explain that I preferred to walk. There was always another day for walking.

We drove for perhaps 3 or 4 kilometres (2 or 3 miles), rising steadily through an old forest of big trees, sometimes glimpsing spectacular views. None of the three men could speak any German, English or French. 'Only Turkish', the driver said, belligerently.

I shrugged and smiled pointing to myself: 'English, I have no Turkish.' Watching this pantomime in the rear mirror the driver wanted to be angry – perhaps he had had a bad day – but then he relented and laughed. They dropped me at the restaurant chalet high in the forest and I sat for an hour drinking beer, smoking and peering between the trees at the distant valley now obscured by an evening heat haze.

I had another 'Thatcher' conversation that evening. When the first ice had been broken, or perhaps as a means of breaking it, Turks would say: *Margaret Tatcheer* and when I had deciphered what they meant – her name gave them considerable pronunciation problems – I would nod and wait. 'Good?' they mighty suggest interrogatively, and depending upon my mood I would either shrug non-committally or more likely shake my head in a violent negative. 'Not good?': they would act surprised but then laugh. Turkish men are essentially 'macho' and the concept of a woman prime minister was not an easy one for them to accept, so that I was never sure in such a male-dominated society whether they had suggested her name in awe, wonder, horror, amazement or contempt for a country whose men allowed a woman to be their prime minister.

I walked back down the hill from the park in the gathering dusk as the lights of Yozgat came on below me. After an indifferent meal I found another tea-garden hidden away in a yard. For a while I sat alone but sensed myself to be under observation and before long two young men invited me to join them. We talked but, as I was beginning to discover, the younger Turks were less interested than their elders is discovering my life-history; instead they wanted to know about Britain or other places where I had travelled, and often they wanted me to be a pen-friend once back in England 'so as to help us learn English'.

Sometimes they asked about the chances of work in Britain and then I had to explain how exceptionally difficult entrance for immigrants seeking work would be. 'But not if we were in the European Community,' they might reply.

'Precisely: that is why we shall keep you out.'

These two were brothers. They wanted me to write when I returned home and we exchanged addresses.

Eventually, when I did get back to Britain and totted up the number of new correspondents I had picked up, to say nothing of the orders for photographs which I had been given, I groaned at the sheer immensity of the new correspondence to which I was committed.

# 27

# Hafik and Sheep

I returned to Sivas from Yozgat by long-distance bus, on which I found what I thought was an empty seat but then a young man came to dispute my possession. In such circumstances I pretend incomprehension – language difficulties can be helpful – and after a while he shrugged and sat beside me, quite friendly. It was a three-hour drive at 80 kilometres (50 miles) an hour for most of the way across the heartland of the ancient Hittite Empire and very nearly the dead centre of Turkey. At Sivas I returned to my former hotel, where they expressed their delight at my reappearance; my pleasure in their pleasure was later tempered by the receptionist's claim that I owed them for an extra day. Only by reference to my diary did I persuade him that he was mistaken.

I spent the remainder of the day sightseeing: Sivas is a lovely town to wander in, doing my laundry, drinking tea. One unforgettable sight was of an ancient arthritic pair: a tiny little old woman almost literally bent double gamely made her way along the side of the street, a thick stick in one hand, a bundle clasped in the other; she was followed by her husband, equally old, small and bent, whose left hand grasped her shawl for guidance so that he had the appearance of actually being pulled along by his more doughty companion, while ineffectually tapping with a large heavy walking-stick that he held in his other hand, the stick more a symbol than a true aid to his progress, which depended upon his spouse's shawl. In the evening I went to the Kosk restaurant where a *Piyanist Santor* entertained the diners. At a table near me was a single woman in a party of men: they were talking English for the benefit of a guest, I think some kind of businessman, and she was clearly loving being a liberated woman. Apart from tourists or visitors the great majority of Turkish diners were always men. Some restaurants had side-rooms for the use of parties accompanied by women so that they could be more private, but women dining on their own I simply did not see.

My journey now took me along he main Sivas to Erzincan road, and for most of it the Kizil Irmak is in sight. Although the river was reduced to little more than a stream I had to remember that it was the end of the summer dry season: during the spring thaws it would be swollen to at least twice the size and along these upper reaches a number of large tributary streams join it from the hills to either side of the broad valley. My next destination was Hafik, some 38 kilometres (23 miles) from Sivas, and I set off to walk although I had awoken with a bad throat. I was on a main road so felt sure that I could obtain a lift if I needed one: the difficulty would be fending them off. When cars stopped ahead of me I would shake my head and wave my hand in a negative sign but that rarely prevented them waiting for me to come up. 'You want to walk?' Amazement and disbelief would be followed by a curiously resigned shrug which I shall forever equate with Turks whom I forced to concede, however reluctantly, my right to walk.

Hafik is a small town, little more than a village, off the main road. It was busy and seemed crowded although much of the business consisted in tea-drinking on the roadside. A substantial proportion of the male population, indeed, seemed to be permanent fixtures at the various tea-houses, all of which I visited. I obtained a room in a tiny hotel that fronted on to the main street and spent some of my time sitting at the window of my room writing, while I watched the street bustle below me. Interestingly in Hafik I found that I could sit in one or other of the tea-houses, or outside them on the street, without being constantly approached and questioned, although I was the recipient of many inquiring glances. This was all the more curious because Hafik very clearly was not a place likely to be visited by tourists, who would motor straight past it on the highway. One passer-by did wish me '*bonjour*' but did not stop to follow up his greeting. I found this readiness to leave me alone a new experience, and despite my occasional irritation at constantly being questioned I now felt almost insulted by not being questioned at all!

From Hafik I followed one of the tributaries towards the village of Cellali some 20 kilometres (12 miles) away. This was a side trip which I made simply because the country looked so appealing. I consulted my ancient Royal Geographical Society maps to be confronted with frequent references to sheepfolds and as I soon discovered that walk took me through the heart of sheep country. All the flocks I saw had just been sheared so that the creatures appeared extra white in their nakedness and huddled close to each other in tight groups for warmth, thus hardly requiring dogs to keep them together. This looked promising: the thought occurred to me that the dogs might be taking their annual holidays! None the less I kept a sharp look-out for attendant Anatolian shepherd dogs, ready for instant evasive action if attacked. Once when I rounded a bluff I saw an outcrop of white rocks which looked suspiciously like sheep, but there was absolutely no movement and after a while I assumed that they really were rocks. Only when I had come within 100 metres did I realise that the rocks were indeed shorn sheep huddling tightly together, all their heads into the centre of the silent flock. No dog appeared and I left them gathered below a tiny shepherd's rock cottage.

I came to a dramatic escarpment rising some hundred metres sheer above the river so I left the road to follow it. Some distance along this I found a convenient knoll and sat watching the plain below. Two distant dust clouds turned into flocks of sheep being driven to the river to be watered; both flocks were liberally sprinkled with black goats. The day was bright and almost cloudless and when they had approached sufficiently near I took some photographs and then sat watching as the shepherds wandered up and down the river-bank checking their flocks. The river was immediately beneath me and from the point where I was sitting I could not see its near bank 90 metres (300 feet) or more below. One of the shepherds, whose two large dogs clearly had the sheep and goats under absolute control, now removed his boots, waded into the river and crossed towards me and out of sight.

I smoked in anticipation and sure enough, perhaps 10 minutes later, he appeared scrambling up the rocks not more than 20 metres (20 yards) from where I sat. He was a youngster of no more than 16 or 17 and showed no sign of breathlessness after what must have been a difficult and extremely steep climb. Intrigued at the sight of a solitary stranger outlined on the top of the escarpment he could not resist an immediate investigation. We smoked and talked in the mixture of languages, signs, and references to map and dictionary which I had now developed, if not to a fine art, at least to a workable means of communication. Then I took his picture, which I promised to send when back in England, and he promptly provided me with his address. He had a splendid name: Nihat Pirendeoglu.

When I returned to Hafik that evening I was greeted many times along the street. Perhaps the earlier reluctance to get into conversation with me in the tea-houses had been no more than the caution of remote people; I was not to know. That evening I dined well in a small *lokanta* which offered soups (various), a superb mutton stew and beer. Then I repaired to the largest of Hafik's tea houses, which was full of men playing *Okey* or backgammon. The host actually turned off the television so uninterested were his clientele, though that action was a rarity I only encountered in one other place. Later in my room, which for once had a bright light that made writing easy, I spent an hour or more on my notes although I was periodically diverted into watching the tea-house across the street where the games continued until late.

# 28

# Zara

The little town of Zara, set in high country surrounded by dramatic hills, has an air about it: it is the end of the road. From the beginning I had regarded Zara as my final destination in following the Kizil Irmak, although I was to go further; it was a convenient name at which to aim and many times in conversation when using my map to assist inadequate language I had pointed to Zara as my ultimate destination. The professor at Haçibektaş had referred to it as a remote place in the mountains, and it certainly had a distinctive character of its own.

By the time I left Hafik for Zara I had come increasingly to abandon planning: I found it paid to do so. As a rule I had a vague plan, but I did what circumstances dictated on the day, and these often varied enormously. I had cleared Hafik by eight in the morning and by the time I had walked 2 kilometres (1 mile) and was back on the main road I came to a sign indicating that Zara was a further 32 kilometres (20 miles) away. I determined that this day I should not succumb to any offers of lifts. It was a lovely stretch of road with magnificent views to either side and my walk was not spoiled despite considerable traffic, the bulk of it consisting of long-distance trucks, often on their way to Iran. After a couple of hours, as I was walking up a steep hill, a small car passed me. It stopped 200 metres ahead, turned and came back. The driver was a man, his companions three women, each with traditional Muslim head-dresses: they were Iranians. Where was I going? Did I not want a lift? – No I did not want a lift and I was following the river. They were delighted, although my explanation took some little time, and then once more the man turned his car and drove off while the three women clapped at me and laughed in amused, genuine pleasure.

That day's walk provided me with a series of images. Once, in mid-morning, I watched a flock of sheep far below me in the valley and as I wondered about their attendant dogs I saw a solitary specimen of gigantic proportions walking up the hill across the road ahead of me. It had clearly come from the flock and was going about some mysterious business of its own – possibly taking a morning break from guard duty – but as it crossed the road and then continued up the hill on the other side it kept stopping to turn and eye me. These highly intelligent dogs like to get high up the better to scent and spot possible enemies. I kept walking and it must have decided that I was no threat to the sheep it had left below, although several times more it turned to check my intentions. Satisfied at last, it had a roll in the grass and then proceeded majestically once more up the hill, along whose skyline there now appeared a horse and cart, perfectly silhouetted, which for 1 kilometre (half a mile) jogged along parallel to the road below before disappearing over the horizon.

Drivers hooted at me as they passed, some adding the curious cupped hand sign of amazed inquiry which I had grown to expect. At noon I came to a garage and large *lokanta* designed principally to deal with the long-distance buses. Men were sitting outside drinking tea and they eyed me speculatively for the few hundred metres I was in sight before I arrived. I had a Fanta followed by a large tea. By then I was about 20 kilometres (12 miles) from Hafik; they thought I was crazy. Later, I rose steadily over a pass: down below was a small lake, its shores white with alkali as the receding waters of summer had left salt sands behind them. At the top of the pass a number of women sat in the shade of a huge rock and for once returned my greeting: there were no men in sight. By one o'clock occasional clouds had passed before the sun to blunt the worst of its heat.

At one stage, while I walked along a stretch of flat country close to the river, a dust cloud across the plain announced the approach of a great flock of sheep being driven to water, but they and their attendant dogs were on the other side of the Kizil Irmak, where I hoped they would remain. Between one and two I lay under a tree for a midday rest. At about four in the afternoon I came to another garage and *lokanta* where I again stopped for refreshment, and got into conversation with two truck drivers who insisted upon following my route on the map, village by village, all the way from the Black Sea. Then I set off, wearily, to cover the last 5 kilometres (3 miles) into Zara. During that final stretch of what had been a long day's walk I developed a blister on my right foot. It was the first I had acquired, and I could feel it becoming larger and more painful as I limped the apparently interminable last 2 kilometres (1 mile) off the main road into Zara. I had had no trouble at all with my feet until then, even at the beginning when I was not in walking practice.

Zara was a mixture. The main road into the town was wide and modern with up-to-date street lighting, a well-kept railed off cemetery, and a big school. Then came the old town, more of a jumble, on several levels and bustling with the beginnings of evening activity, when everything comes to life again. I found a small, pleasant-looking hotel; in the reception area an old man promised that someone would come to attend to me, but I had to wait for 15 minutes before a rather simple youth appeared and he went through the slow business of transposing information from my passport into the hotel register. He and the old man then accompanied me upstairs to a room with its own shower and lavatory. This did not work well so they transferred me to another room and promptly disappeared. The shower in that room did not work at all so I went downstairs and persuaded them to put me back in the first room. By then I was expert at manipulating Turkish showers and getting the best out of them. I changed and showered, exhausted by about 35 kilometres (22 miles) of walking, before setting off to find a *Fici Bira* sign: I was thirsty and limping now from my blister, which was a good 4 cm (inch and a half) across.

There was a large beer sign just across the street but I had to go down some dark steps into a cavernous underground shopping mall, most of whose shops were as yet unoccupied, although no doubt waiting for prosperity and customers to come. The pub was dark but pleasant. I flopped into a seat and downed my first beer in two minutes, my second in five and then sat over a third beer, my thirst from one of the longest, hottest and hardest day's walks I could remember finally slaked. Later I limped round the centre of the town in the gathering dusk to get the feel of it, had a meal in a busy friendly *lokanta* and then returned to the beer parlour, where I had a *raqi*. The host sent me a dish of complimentary melon to go with it and another man sent me a dish of nuts. Strangers, it seemed, were rare and welcome. I got into conversation with two men at an adjoining table but soon excused myself on the grounds of exhaustion after an exceptionally long day – they were suitably impressed that I had walked from Hafik – and returned to my hotel, where I spent a rotten night with a rapidly developing cold going to throat and chest.

I was not going anywhere the next day, as apart from a blistered foot I had developed a bad throat. I limped around the little town, bought some marvellous-looking peaches, two of which turned out to be bad and then found a chemist and with the aid of sign language obtained Benylin for my cold.

It is amazing how easy it is to muddle up a river, though one might not think so. The Kizil Irmak runs parallel to the main highway 2 or so kilometres (1 mile) from the town, but a tributary of the same size runs through Zara, and I spent time contemplating this from the bridge in the centre of the town while women did their washing on its banks, where large straw mats or cloths were laid out, covered with freshly harvested wheat spread on them to dry. Only later did I sort out the two rivers to my satisfaction: at first I mistook this for the Kizil Irmak.

Coming back across the bridge towards the centre of the town I met several policemen setting off on their morning duties. One greeted me and I discovered that he spoke very good English: 'It is not often I have the opportunity to talk with an Englishman,' he said, 'would you mind spending some time with me later in the day so that I can practise?'

'Indeed, why not,' I said.

'Eleven o'clock in the police station?' he suggested.

'Fine,' I agreed. I continued my limp round the town. A conversation with a friendly policeman who spoke such good English would be entertaining and instructive. Had I detected just a hint of an order?

I might have been some kind of police inspector-general judging by the reception I received at the police station. My English-speaking friend welcomed me and I was introduced to several of his colleagues, each of whom then constituted an audience to our conversation, chiefly to make fun of my host's English. But, undaunted, the two of us proceeded to hold a wide-ranging discussion, as the politicians like to say, covering Turkey and the European Community, poverty and Turkey's position between the Third World and Europe, the fact that Turkish people are not ecology-conscious, the place of Islam in Turkish society, the large wheat surplus, European opposition to Turkey joining the Community on the grounds that it is a peasant society. Other policemen came and went while this discussion continued, some contributing to it, others merely acting as spectators. After about half an hour my host inquired whether I would like some refreshment and two huge ripe melons were procured and sliced up. It was some of the sweetest melon I had tasted up to that time.

We continued our conversation. The Turks, my host suggested, want to be regarded as European but in fact are mainly Asian, the country acting as a bridge between two worlds. They are very conscious of any rejection by Europe, and constantly seek to prove themselves acceptable to Europe; it is certainly the case that the lure of Europe is at present very strong in much of the country. This conversation, one of the most enlightening I had, spread over an hour. Then, with the greatest possible courtesy, my policeman host murmured that he would just like a look at my passport. He had certainly chosen an elegant way of going about his job. He thumbed through this, remarking on the other countries I had visited while he failed to find the Turkish entry stamp. I was not really surprised, merely pleased at the gentlemanly way the demand for the passport had been presented. Zara is off the tourist track and by then, with two months' growth of beard and clothes which obstinately refused to demonstrate more than a semblance of cleanliness, I must have presented a fairly bizarre appearance. He had early paid attention to my beard, which I had described as my 'Turkey' beard.

I do not believe in coddling myself when ill, and despite the cold and the blister I decided to walk the hills behind the town that afternoon. The best way to get my foot back into action was to walk on the blister; the throat and cold would simply have to run their course. So I set off up a gully which came down to the road near the point where I had entered the town the day before. My cold, however, fairly rapidly brought me out in a violent sweat even though I was deliberately going quite slowly, so I paused to rest and at once I heard a deep-throated growl. It was undoubtedly one of those damned dogs and sure enough it appeared: a small, floppy, enchanting puppy which could hardly have been more than two months old but was already getting into practice with its growl. No irate protective bitch appeared to guard her young but I at once continued up the steep hill: she might materialise at any moment.

The view from the top was magnificent and as always the weather gave a sharp, distant edge to visibility. At the other end of the hill which runs parallel to the road through Zara the descent was even more rocky and steep. I had not gone very far when a furious barking greeted me: three Anatolian shepherd dogs were watching me from the entrance to what looked like a small scooped out hillside cave. One was a large female on the verge of whelping, the second remained majestically seated and only one smallish male stood to the front barking and wagging his tail. Had I produced some meat I think he would have been quite friendly.

When I eventually got down to the valley at the end of the town – a part I had not yet visited – two men appeared from their cottages, curious as ever, to ask who I was, where I came from, and what I was doing, so we stood chatting for a while before I walked back into the centre of town. Later I encountered a group of women who also wished to know what I was doing. This was sufficiently rare to be an occasion, so I stopped to exchange greetings. That morning, in fact, just before my encounter with the police a woman had greeted me in French. After I had eaten I went to the pub, where I was questioned by several men in turn; they also offered me beer. I was developing into something of a fixture!

# 29

# Imranli and
# the Head of the River

The road from Zara to Imranli is spectacular: it winds along the hillside high above the river which twists and loops in its valley below with an escarpment rising sheer on the far side. I had walked about 15 kilometres (9 miles) – there was very little traffic for it was a Sunday – when my blistered foot began to trouble me again and as though by design one of the long-distance buses came by and, much to my amazement, stopped to take me on board. I was found a seat near the back and promptly put to the question by the curious passengers. A man with passable French and a second man with some English led the questioning, while others fed them with queries of their own. They were intrigued to see me walking along this unlikely stretch of road: where did I come from and where was I going? Who was I, why was I in Turkey at all, what did I think of it? and so on for the rest of the ride to Imranli. I explained about my river journey and this heightened their interest. Someone from the front of the bus sent back a plate of grapes for me. The French-speaking man delicately inquired about my clothes. I was wearing a pair of trousers, once fawn but now grey, and a wind-jacket, both of them the worse for wear, and the jacket more or less permanently stained on the back from the sweat and friction of my rucksack. 'Why are your clothes so . . .' he paused but could find no euphemism, 'dirty?' he inquired. I explained that two months' walking with a minimum of gear and only one change meant that smartness was not possible. I might have added that washing facilities in most of the hotels where I had stayed were at best totally inadequate, and often made cleaning, except at a most rudimentary level, an unrewarding exercise. When we reached Imranli I offered to pay but they would have none of it: the lift was courtesy of the bus company.

Imranli was rather like an alpine village in Switzerland. It had a pretty open square which contained four small hotels but not much else. The hills rose stark and beautiful behind it. I wandered round simply looking but some old men outside a tea-house demanded why: 'The road is back there', and they pointed the way I had just come. I often found that in small places like this people could not understand why I should want to look round: partly such incomprehension was genuine – they did not believe there was anything of interest for me to see and so assumed that I was looking for the obvious, a *lokanta* or the road; and partly it was something quite different – the reluctance of peasants to have a stranger 'probing' their small community. When I was accosted in this manner I made a point of explaining carefully what I was doing; it was part of the balance which had to be maintained between their curiosity and potential resentment of the stranger against my desire to see a new place – all of it – rather than simply the obvious sights, assuming that there were any 'sights' at all in such tiny places.

From Imranli I went walking. There are two streams, head-waters of the river, which join together at Zara but by Imranli they have diverged: one rises on the slopes of Bey Dagi, south-east of Zara and about 20 kilometres (12 miles) in a straight line from Imranli; the other continues somewhat further east along the line of the highway before it also turns south from its source in another part of the same range of hills. The weather was clear and bright, the hills very beautiful if bleak countryside exercises an appeal as it does for me. In the valleys trees and streams rendered everything more gentle. But I often found myself wondering what these hills would be like in winter when snow and the extreme temperatures for which Turkey is famous have descended on the land.

I kept a constant look-out for sheep – there were plenty of flocks about – although it was the dogs that concerned me. Once I came upon a relaxed bucolic scene: a number of Turkish families had driven out in tractors and trailers to a little meadow beside the river where they were enjoying a picnic. It looked like some kind of celebration, and I might have joined it had not a number of guard dogs come barking towards me. So I waved and veered back towards the line of hills I had been following. I did not reach the actual springs or begin-nings of either tributary but then I had not set myself any such stern target. In any case, as I have long since discovered, most rivers are boring where they begin: a tiny trickle of water seeps out of an improb-able place on an unimpressive hillside, giving little or no indication of the mighty river to come, so I did not feel I would miss anything spectacular. I did, however, enjoy walking those hills, which proved easier underfoot than the road had been, so that my blister though still troublesome began, as I hoped, to 'harden' away.

Not only does Turkey provide a stunning landscape; it is also a geographer's paradise, presenting an endless succession of cols, saddles, striated rock, moraines and other classic examples of land features that I had learnt in my schooldays and subsequently forgotten. Most of these, moreover, were in pristine condition: not just a saddle but a perfect example of a saddle.

When I had finished walking the hills I had to return to Zara before crossing the divide to follow the Yeşil Irmak back to the Black Sea. I took a bus back to Zara, mainly to save my foot but also because I should be covering old ground again. I had to take my chance at the bus station since I had not made a booking, with the result that when one of the big buses called on its way to Sivas and Ankara I found every seat was booked. I got into conversation with one of the passengers, a tall young man with an Australian accent who had spent seven years in Australia. He was back in Turkey to visit his mother, who was with him on the bus. He had no illusions about Turkey. He began by asking what I thought of it but after a short time listening to my praises he interrupted. Turkey, he said, was very poor, its people were oppressed – sometimes by the government, sometimes by the rich. Many people were without jobs and had no prospects of future employment. The long winters were bitter and then there was nothing to do. Moreover, despite the impressions I might have obtained, the Turkish people were not helpful. With me it was curiosity rather than a desire to help that prompted their interest. Australia, he continued, was quite different. There people were genuinely helpful. 'It is all very well for you to come here on a visit and say how pleasant it is but you do not have to live here', he concluded.

He spoke with considerable bitterness about Turkey and with the fervour of a convert about Australia. He had only come back to see his mother and, if he could arrange for her to come out to him in Sydney, he said he had no intention of returning to Turkey. His mother stood by smiling happily at him while he spoke to me: she had only Turkish. His younger brother was also there, and he was going to accompany him back to Australia. As ever it was a question of immigrant visas. I should have liked to follow up this conversation for he was both bitter and forthright in what he had to say and though I had had some interesting conversations about the country and its politics had never spoken to anyone who went so near the knuckle to a stranger. But the big bus was about to depart so we shook hands and they went, leaving me to investigate transport for myself.

I found a lift to Zara almost at once: one of the little buses normally used on local routes drew up at the bus station. It was empty apart from the driver and two men sitting at the front with him, one of whom spoke English and had worked for six years in the Gulf. The bus was going to Sivas and they would drop me at the end of the main highway. The driver had the most astonishing black hair I have ever seen: thick, glossy, but from natural oil, with huge black eyebrows which met in a straight line above his eyes, a large, perfectly trained walrus moustache and two days' growth of beard. The combination gave him a raffish yet somehow formidable air. They wanted tea before continuing their journey and I joined them. Then after 20 minutes we set off, although in fact they made a diversion for my benefit and drove across the old road which had been the main route before the construction of the highway to set me down in the centre of Zara. I paid the driver TL 2,000.

I returned to the same hotel in Zara, where I received a warm welcome and was given my old room, whose window proved an excellent vantage point from which to take photographs of the street scene below although I was spotted doing this by a woman at the door of a big corner house on the opposite side of the street. Thereafter, every time she came to her front door she would look cautiously towards my window before proceeding with her business. Much passed below me: an old high-sided wooden cart with block wheels full of wheat and pulled by two bullocks; old men talking; a woman with shawl drawn tight round her face stepping out with long strides like a man; a tractor and trailer with the whole family on the back, all in thick clothes against the cold of the early morning as they set off for the fields.

In the dark beer house that evening I had a curious encounter. I was sitting in my usual place, back to the wall, when a large man I had already spoken to on other occasions came to sit beside me. He had reasonable French and we chatted casually, but then he took my notebook from me – I had been writing – and began to go through it. I took it back from him. At first he looked angry, then baffled, then he smiled and shrugged. It was hard not to be angry with such over-inquisitiveness but I did my best. I also had to draw a line at some point; in his case I could not rid myself of the idea that he was some kind of policeman.

After a while he got up and left: I think I had succeeded in embarrassing him, which if true was certainly unusual. Now a man on my other side got into conversation with me. He was 57, so he said, and had a little German which he employed in a form of shorthand: '*Deutschland*

– *viele geld'*, he might say, and throw back his head to laugh, at which I would nod. Then he would leave me in peace for three or four minutes before venturing another reflection: 'Germans are clever', or 'Germany is capitalist', a comment that brought forth the largest of his guffaws. The evening in the pub ended with a fight. Without prior noise or argument two men were suddenly on their feet shouting. It looked ugly and I was interested to see the speed with which the proprietor was joined by two other men to break it up. They locked one man away in a little side room where he banged on the door and shouted, and they put the other out. Later the two came back to be reconciled. I had no idea what it was about. In the *lokanta* where I took supper I met my policeman friend again and we talked about minorities. If I were to believe him they are all content: Arab, Jew, Armenian, Greek and even the five million Kurds; I was not entirely convinced. A waiter came up to tell me that his uncle worked in a restaurant in Tottenham. The policeman sent him away brusquely; I think the poor man wanted me to take greetings to his relation.

Various people had pointed out to me that Turkey is a poor country which suffers from civil and human rights oppressions. It is still, despite its yearning to be included in the European Community, a Third World country. I had been especially struck by the vehemence of the young Turk from Australia whom I met at Imranli. I had not come to Turkey to look at social or political problems although these always interest me. Instead I had made a point of taking the country and its people as I found them, and for me at least their generous qualities outweighed many of the faults of which I was subconsciously aware.

My blistered foot was only partly better despite my policy of hardening it by use and I knew I could not do any serious walking for a day or so. This helped persuade me to change my plans. My original intention had been to take the road north from Zara to Serefiye and then to turn west and follow the Yeşil Irmak down its valley to the dam and reservoir by Almus before I reached Tokat. I now decided to take in an extra valley and continue from Serefiye to Suşehri on the Kelkit river, a long tributary which joins the Yeşil Irmak below the town of Erbaa. The Kelkit valley, so I had learnt, is of spectacular beauty and I would follow it to Niksar (New Caesarea) and then cut across to Tokat and the Yeşil Irmak. By doing this I would take in an additional stretch of territory. Whatever I intended to do the next stage of my journey had to be by bus because of my foot: the stretch of road from Zara to Suşehri covers 72 kilometres (45 miles) and includes the Karabayir pass at 1,925 metres (6,315 feet).

148

My hotel had cost me an absurd price of less than 1 pound sterling a day and I had enjoyed it. The morning of my departure for Suşehri I had breakfast of soup in a little *lokanta* on the main road. Half-way through my meal the man at the next table gave an ear-splitting whistle which had the effect of bringing a huge passing truck to a standstill. He went across the road to obtain a lift to work. I missed one bus to Suşehri since it simply swept past the tea-house where it was supposed to stop and continued majestically on its way. When I asked in the little ticket office why this should have been they merely shrugged. So I spent several hours in the tea-house and was not sorry to do so for this was a splendid one to study.

The tea-house provides a marvellous microcosm of (male) Turkish life. Endless teas are served at absurdly low prices, sometimes for as little as TL 30 or 40 a glass. This was an especially busy establishment and at a conservative estimate I decided it would serve a minimum of 2,000 teas in a day. At TL 50 a glass that would be TL 100,000 or 70 pounds sterling. The tea-house, like an English pub, is a meeting place. It has its quota of old men, permanent fixtures, who spend the better part of their day in it. Often men would peer in to see whether a friend was there or whether it looked active and interesting enough to warrant their remaining. Some came to play games: *Okey*, backgammon, cards or dominoes. *Okey* intrigued me but I suppose that was because I did not know the rules and it looked different from anything with which I was acquainted.

The tea-house is also a place of business. The shoeshine boys with their wooden rests slung by a strap from the shoulder come round in an endless stream, two or three at a time, touting for custom. I was not bothered by them for my walking boots were of a peculiar brown and I waxed them myself. They would take one look and then reluctantly pass by, not even attempting their normal arts of persuasion upon me. Sometimes the proprietor or the tea boy would drive them out but a new lot would come a few moments later and every so often, for the clientele was constantly changing, they would discover a new customer. A man who sat for an hour or more in a tea-house could easily be approached a dozen times by shoeshine boys of various sizes – the youngest were no more than seven or eight, the oldest in their early teens.

It is a place of constant motion: people would change from one table to another as they moved between their friends; newcomers would do the rounds greeting acquaintances, a group at a table would shuffle chairs round to make a place for a newcomer and when someone got up to leave his friends might rise to kiss him on the cheeks before he departed. It was interesting to watch the arrival of a newcomer at a table where four or five men were already established. He might greet the first person with a kiss on both cheeks, give the second a warm handshake, the third and fourth a more perfunctory handshake, the fifth a nod. Thus the degree of acquaintance could be gauged. Sometimes a man came simply to sit and waved away the offer of tea; he merely wanted company or a place to rest. Certainly it was my experience that once I had purchased an initial tea I could sit more or less for ever, although in my case I had developed such a thirst that I was always a good source of business, consuming at least three glasses of tea over half an hour and often four or five.

A busy house needs a large supply of glasses for as well as its immediate guests it will service half the town or at least the neighbouring shops and *lokantas* as well. In this case men or boys from nearby shops would come to the window, tap to gain the attention of the tea boy and then display two, three or four fingers before disappearing; the boy would then take that number of glasses across the street. This particular house provided lemon and apple as well as ordinary tea, and by ten-thirty in the morning it was crowded, the noise deafening, rather like a London pub on a Friday evening.

I watched a thickset old blind man being led from across the busy street to the entrance of the tea-house. After feeling the door jamb to be sure of his bearings he produced a begging cup and then slowly, meticulously, worked his way round the large room from table to table holding out his cup. He had come at the right time and made a good collection.

The tea-house was also a popular unloading place: tractors and trailers, often with a complement of people, would stop just outside, and when the passengers had alighted and secured their bundles many would head for the tea-house to have a drink or meet friends before going about their affairs. Most of the men wore cloth caps; the women always, as far as I could see, wore headscarves here and frequently covered their mouths. One tractor and trailer looked as though it had come a long distance for the children were all covered in dust and when they got down their mother took a rag to wipe their faces. In another trailer a heifer managed to get its head stuck in an opening between the boards and then proceeded to bellow for 20 minutes before anybody thought to do anything about it. A boy stood before the tea-house eating hard green pears, his face twisted by the sourness but determined to continue anyway.

The long road to Serefiye and on to Suşehri proved to be the most exciting I travelled. The bus left Zara along the green valley into which I had descended from my walk in the hills above the town, but almost at once we began to rise, twisting and turning our way up into ever bleaker hills. We doubled back on our track along hairpin bends with the valley precipitously below us, tiny villages on the opposite hillsides apparently only approached by tracks. There were plenty of sheep about and had I been walking I have no doubt I should have had more than one encounter with their guard dogs. We dropped through a dramatic gorge and then rose again before we reached Serefiye. Thereafter the journey became even more dramatic: the hills became starker, the distant prospects were shrouded in cloud and we climbed to the pass of Karabayir before descending towards the distant, apparently straight mountain range which ran along the far side of the Kelkit valley towards which we were driving. Suşehri is built on a hill, the valley of the Kelkit below it.

# 30

# The Kelkit Valley

Personal obstinacies take strange forms. At one level I did not mind travelling by bus – I had done so on a number of previous occasions – but I did mind if I felt I had to do so. The moment I arrived at Suşehri I regretted that I had not walked that marvellous road over the divide and determined that I should walk the next stretch whatever the condition of my foot.

There was a convenient tea-house by the bus-stop where I alighted in Suşehri and next door to it a small hotel. I took tea with my map spread out on the table so that I could satisfy the curiosity of two or three neighbours from the next table and then the proprietor asked whether I wanted a hotel. At my affirmative nod he went away to return with an old man who ran the establishment next door – they were uncle and nephew, I think – and as a result of his convenient appearance I decided to stay there instead of wandering the town to inspect alternative accommodation. My tea was on the house. I have no doubt that the tea-house proprietor got other custom for his uncle's hotel in this way. The old man took me upstairs to a tiny room without any washing facilities but with a superb view across the valley below to the mountains on the other side. That view compensated for any other inconvenience, even the plumbing arrangements, which left a good deal to the imagination.

Suşehri is an exciting little town perched on the edge of a steep descent into the river valley. Behind my hotel was a street concerned solely with mechanics, which meant the repair of tractors and farm implements. Like ancient Athens, with streets set aside for different trades, I came upon this arrangement in many towns. This was an especially dramatic street, every shop-front open so that the interior formed a garage with pit to take in vehicles for repair; the noise was deafening, almost everything was liberally smeared with oil or grease, and the shops had the appearance of dark caverns with black-faced mechanics busy in their depths.

On a steep hill I took a photograph of a curious cockeyed building whose upper storey looked as though it was about to collapse, and the man by whose shop I had stopped to do this promptly invited me to take tea with him. A stool was brought, tea arrived almost at once from a neighbouring tea-house and a small crowd gathered round to talk with the stranger and relieve the boredom of the day. They seemed particularly interested when they established that I was English rather than German, and as usual I provided a potted history of myself and my doings in Turkey. Then I continued to wander.

I visited another tea-house, where a momentary silence descended at my appearance. An old man behind a market stall called 'Monsieur' and came to shake my hand: he had no language to offer except Turkish and did not appear to want to talk anyway. His teeth were all silver. Two men poured cement in a primitive yet effective way: one stood on a platform half-way up what was to be a cement pillar with four boards bound in place by string round the core of iron stakes. The second man brought a wheelbarrow to the base of this rising pillar and with a superb sweeping motion, forming a perfect arc each time round, shovelled cement from it up on to the platform, which was above the level of his head. There his partner scooped up the cement with a large trowel as fast as it arrived and flipped it into the hollow made by the boards until the wheelbarrow was empty and the cement had exactly reached the top of the boards: a prime example of perfect calculation.

I ate in the same place more than once and on my second appearance they treated me as an *habitué* and showed me to a place with a flourish. There was a charming tea-garden in the centre of the town. For a while I sat in peace, alone, but I was aware of an old man eyeing me from a nearby table; eventually he could stand it no longer and came across to greet me and talk. I offered him a cigarette, which he took with trembling hands; we were then joined by another old man, his friend, and the three of us sat in amicable silence until we were joined by a young man with a little English. His arrival allowed me to tell them of my journey so far to Suşehri, which was what they wanted to hear. They were delighted and suddenly, in the two old men with weather-beaten faces and walrus moustaches, and the young man assiduously poised between them to interpret, I saw a superb photographic portrait, yet when I asked if I could take a picture they declined with an almost feminine bashfulness. It was the first time that men had ever refused to be photographed. The young man, perhaps in compensation for their refusal, ordered a Coke for me – a drink I abominate as I feel any reasonable person must, but I was obliged to drink it. He was a student at the *Lisee*. I offered further cigarettes: the first old man declined to take another, but the second man accepted one. When I left there were salaams all round; I returned to my hotel to do some writing.

I went walking in the stark hills across the valley, zigzagging up a road of hairpin bends and the nearer I got to the apparent top of the hill the steeper the going became. I was in no hurry and more than once walked out on to a bluff to survey the scene below or take a photograph. Far below me I could see two figures, little more than black dots, on the road I had come up. The uniform darkness of their clothes suggested that they were policemen and with an instinct which had nothing to do with any observable movement I knew they were watching me and interested to know more. They left the road below and took to a track I had seen on my way up which soon disappeared from sight behind a shoulder of hill. I recalled that whereas my road zigzagged that path went up almost vertically.

I continued walking and after another hairpin bend, just as I approached a near horizon, the two policemen erupted from behind the hill. They must have been going at a considerable pace to catch up with me so quickly, despite the fact that I had not been hurrying. The older man looked abashed at coming so unexpectedly face to face with me and hastily turned his back to sit down on the bank – they had appeared at a distance of about 50 metres – while the younger simply walked on as though they were about some quite other business. I hailed them and they turned and came to greet me. They must both have been in remarkably good condition for neither appeared to be breathing hard from their rapid climbing exertions: the smaller and older man, of perhaps 35, looked a formidable character; the younger and taller, in his twenties, equally tough in a simpler fashion. Both, I noticed, carried rubber truncheons which they had doubled round, clipping the loop of leather attached to the handle over the business end of the truncheon so that it formed a ring which they slipped over the wrist.

My greeting absolved them from embarrassment since I made plain that I had expected them. We sat under a solitary, small, thick-leaved tree and I showed them my map and described my journey. They offered me cigarettes and later, after an amusing conversation where for once I had the advantage, a slight edge derived from catching them in too obvious a demonstration of inquisitiveness, I took their photograph and promised to send them copies from England. Then they turned round and disappeared down the steep path up which they had come while I returned the way I had come. I was not sure whether it had simply been an excess of curiosity or whether their duties as policemen included checking upon strange walkers. But that was not the end of police for the day.

Back at the bottom of the hill I sat on a rock smoking by a pretty little open cemetery. Almost at once a car appeared from a nearby dirt road to draw up beside me. There were three men in it and they offered me a lift, a little imperiously, I thought. I was constantly being frustrated in my walks by the offer of lifts but I usually accepted since such encounters often produced interesting results. Suşehri was maybe 5 or 6 kilometres (3 or 4 miles) distant, at least if we had followed my original path back, but that was not possible since I had taken tracks unsuitable for cars. Instead they went a longer way round and then, when we got on to the main road which they ought to have followed, they went up a dirt side road and then stopped. The driver got out to stretch his legs and the man beside me also got out. The third man in the front seat now produced a pistol which he proceeded to load. I felt slightly nervous at this; it seemed remarkably like an American gangster film in which I was cast as the victim who was about to be shot. The other two men then got back into the car and the driver, who saw me watching the pistol in the driving mirror, said something to his companion, who promptly took out his wallet and produced an identification card: 'I am a policeman', he said, and passed his card to the driver. He and then the other man studied this card as though they had not known their friend's occupation and then passed it to me. It did indeed inform me that Devat Bulut was a policeman. A large empty truck now came along the dirt road towards the turn-off where we were parked. It stopped; the driver got out to greet the three men and knelt by the open driver's door of the car, where a lot of fiddling which I could not see took place, and then he got up to go. Something had changed hands. The driver now gave him a packet of biscuits; he inquired about me and was clearly relieved at the word '*Ingiltere*', which seemed to satisfy him for he came round to shake hands and then returned to his truck and drove off. 'Our' business concluded we drove back to the main road and on to Suşehri, where they dropped me in the main street. Something of a less than honest nature, I felt, had just been transacted. It had been an altogether curious encounter.

After an attempted clean-up in the hotel I returned to the tea-house garden in the centre of the town. A plague of small boys came to annoy me and one, the smallest, sat beside me desperately shy, trying for more than five minutes while his mates goaded him on until at last he plucked up courage and in a strangled voice said: '*What is your name?*' Then an especially unkempt man wandered over and helped himself to one of my cigarettes without asking, casually demanded where I was going and then ambled away. Next came a squat idiot youth with a huge mouth of great teeth set in a permanent grin; I had watched his progress from table to table round the garden. He would examine whoever sat drinking tea and then throw back his head to make an incomprehensible remark. He was always received kindly. Now he had reached me, and after a long examination said something extra loud and wandered off. I noticed that the Turks round the garden were all watching to see how I would react.

That evening I found a new, superior *lokanta* for supper. The proprietor saw me coming and was at the door to greet me; the dining-room was elegantly decorated in fawn and white wallpaper with two shades of wood panelling up to waist height and a number of pictures round the walls; a tape played Mozart. The proprietor had worked in a restaurant in Istanbul, he told me, but had missed Suşehri so had returned to set up business in his home-town. I had an excellent supper of beefsteak, yoghurt and Turkish coffee for TL 1,000. Over my coffee I reflected upon the techniques of the Turkish police. My encounters with them had all been pleasant but there was an interesting efficiency about them: the English speaker in Zara entertaining me so elegantly before asking to see my passport, or the two that afternoon racing up the hill to intercept and check upon a stranger – in retrospect I was quite sure it was not simply curiosity that had impelled them. I was not sure about the man with the gun, but just after the patrol had picked me up we had passed the two policemen from the hill and a signal had passed between them. Once they had established that I was only a harmless foreigner they were courteous beyond words.

From Suşehri to Niksar the long straight valley of the Kelkit covered 122 kilometres (76 miles), although the road did plenty of winding as well as rising steeply up and down many times. I walked much of it but had some lifts as well. There were plenty of sheep and their attendant dogs but I had no trouble with these. The hills were dramatically stark, purple and yellow stone predominating. The river was nearly always in sight, sometimes flowing a mere 9 metres (30 feet) below the road, at other points several hundred metres down a steep cliff as the road wound along the mountainside.

## The Kelkit Valley

At Koyulhisar a new hotel had just been opened with *Turist* standard rooms and hot water in the showers. It was a charming little town and several men in the hotel including the manager befriended me. In the lounge I had begun to write up my diary but that was a mistake for I at once attracted an audience and instead had to provide the history of my travels once more: I was coming to know them by heart. The hotel did not provide beer but one of my audience said he would take me to the pub and we set off up the steep hill to a newly opened establishment where, for once, I managed to pay for a round although it was hard work to persuade my guide, Aziz, to accept a drink from me.

On our way back to the hotel we dropped in at a tea-house. I was introduced as from England and about six men joined our table. One spoke some English and told me that he had a brother in London while another man with a craggy face, reminiscent of Trevor Howard, had flown jets for ten years in the Turkish air force. He and his brother came from Bala so I told them the story of the seven dogs, which was received with great appreciation. I felt like a medieval minstrel retelling my story at each stop, embellishing and refining the details until it was in a suitable form to set to music. Then Aziz and I returned to my hotel, where I had a second hot shower before bed.

Once, on a *dolmus* ride down the valley, we stopped at a water pump for it was an unbearably hot day and everyone got out to drink. We happened to be high up the hillside, the river cataracting over boulders hundreds of metres below us. A superior, well-dressed man now approached and asked if I should like to have my photograph taken – I had just taken a shot of the gorge – and he obliged. Then I lined up the entire complement of the little bus, much to their delight, and took a picture of them all.

The Kelkit must have taken millennia to wear through those granite hills; what was surprising was the straight nature of its course. It is not often that a river runs for such a distance with so few twists or deviations. My foot seemed finally to have recovered but I was quite happy to accept a lift for the last dozen kilometres into Niksar, for the valley finally opened out and the road became far less interesting.

# 31

# Niksar

Niksar was the third name applied to this ancient town, which was formerly the Roman Neocaesarea, although that name was only given to the Pontic town of Cabeira after Pontus had been finally subdued and incorporated into the Roman Empire in the first century of the present era. The town is on the Kelkit Cayi (the ancient Lycus), which I had been following for the last few days, although it would be more accurate to say that the town rises above the river up its steep hillside to the citadel.

I was now very much in the centre of what had been the kingdom of Pontus; this rose to importance under the first Mithridates in the fourth century BC and was to continue as a state for over two centuries before the whole region came under Roman control. Pontus was protected by its mountain ranges and almost every one of the Pontic towns was built round an impressive citadel whose fortress remains still exist today although they have been rebuilt by the Byzantines and then the Seljuks. Pontus rose to its greatest heights under Mithridates VI whose remarkable reign lasted for 57 years before he took his own life in 63 BC rather than become a Roman prisoner. He fought three wars against Rome, providing some of the stiffest resistance to its expansion before all Anatolia finally came under its control. In 62 BC Pontus was proclaimed a Roman Province.

Niksar had been one of the Pontic strongholds in which Mithridates VI Eupator was besieged more than once during his turbulent military career. The remains of the fortress still stand on the citadel while below the modern town straggles up and down steep hills which display a medley of varied buildings, a complete mix of old and new. The main street was being relaid in blocks. Niksar is an exciting place in which to walk, with narrow, steep lanes winding downwards from the principal street, a lively market doing its business beside the deep-cut banks of a small swift stream which runs through the centre of the town and also appears to do service as a sewer.

I found an average-looking '*Hotel Turistik*' whose glass door on to the street, however, was locked. I rang the bell and must have spent ten minutes there before a woman peered down the stairs at me only to disappear again. But she opened the door electronically from above and I went up to a first-floor reception desk. This receptionist was a gaunt, grim woman (unusual for a Turkish hotel), like a concierge's wife in a French novel. I asked for a room with shower and the woman disappeared to the floor above. After another considerable wait a man came to take me upstairs, where we waited in a corridor for the woman, who was busy in a room which I assumed she was preparing for my use. Eventually she appeared but motioned me back angrily when I went to enter; instead she went to a cupboard at the end of the corridor to return with a huge plastic bowl which she took into the room. At the very moment that the man told me there was no water we heard the gushing sound of water, presumably running into the bowl. At last the woman came out to motion me into the bedroom. There was a huge water cylinder in the bathroom which was just inside the entrance and the woman had been running water from this into the plastic bowl. A plastic jug stood beside the bowl and the man signalled that I could take a shower by dipping and douching. Then they left me. I had not wanted a shower at that moment but they had worked so hard to make one available that I took it anyway.

A considerable amount of civic improvement appeared to be in progress apart from the relaying of the roads with squiggle-edged stone blocks, and more than once I came upon road sweepers – not the commonest of sights in some of the places I had visited. I found a tea-house whose first-floor veranda provided a perfect vantage-point for watching the centre of town where the main road which came up from the valley below opened out into a broad square. Niksar was a town in layers: parallel roads at different levels were connected by little streets, alleys or steps. After a considerable search I found a pleasant *restoran* which served beer – it had the *Fici Bira* sign outside – and there too I was able to sit on a veranda watching the bustle below. I did a good deal of sitting in Niksar, drinking tea or beer, and realised that I was physically quite tired.

On both the tea-house and *restoran* verandas I was, as usual, subjected to the questioning to which I had long since become accustomed, but that did not prevent it from sometimes also becoming wearisome. After 20 minutes of dialogue over my first beer the proprietor and the young man who had served me finally let me to myself but, as though sensing that I had wished to be left in peace in the first place, the waiter now returned to give me a present, a compensation for my patience with their inquisition. He brought me a picture frame which he had made out of Pall Mall cigarette boxes; it was a curious, ingenious affair which must have taken time and patience to put together so I thanked him, suitably impressed, and put it in my bag.

In the centre of town I visited a small, Seljuk mosque and, unusually, I was followed round inside by a hovering attendant who watched suspiciously until I had finished my inspection; then he went to the microphone and I realised he had been waiting for me to go so that he could call the faithful to prayer. The finely-carved portal in familiar stalagmite form was an elegant example of Seljuk art and I went to take a picture. A group of boys immediately stood in front of it, pointing to themselves as subject-matter but, happily, three old men who were sitting nearby shooed the boys away and then straightened themselves up to peer solemnly at the camera for me to take their portraits instead. I had only wanted the door.

Niksar was a busy place. Near the outskirts of the town I watched farmers arriving with produce for the next day's market. A little old woman came striding towards me leading a donkey piled high with a load of vegetable matter – I could not distinguish what it was – but as soon as she caught sight of me she pulled her headscarf across her mouth and clamped part of it firmly between her teeth. A photograph would have been out of the question although she would have made a marvellous picture.

On my way from the hotel to a *restoran* where I intended to eat I was called aside by a man supervising repairs to the front of his shop. He spoke good German and was friendly in a more sophisticated way than many of my normal interrogators. He sent for tea and a chair and the two of us, attended by sundry extras, sat on the pavement watching the world go by and talking. He did not want to know my life story but instead talked of Turkey's commercial opportunities or lack of them. I remarked that he seemed to be doing quite well to which he responded with a laugh to say it was possible to do well if you worked hard: 'Like Mrs *Tatcheer* tells you in England?' He was indulging his humour, but then we were interrupted by one of his assistants – some problem to do with the construction going on in the shop had arisen. He invited me to call for a drink later that evening and I continued to the *restoran* I had chosen for my supper.

This was a superior place and the food was excellent. At the end of a leisurely meal I ordered a *raqi;* that must have been the signal, for a group of men at a neighbouring table then insisted I should join them. They were businessmen or friends who had not met in a long time for the three of them were already well advanced into their cups. We had an amusing series of discussions, broken by constant interruptions as others came to our table to greet the men, one of whom I gathered was a civic figure of some importance. Finally I escaped and returned to my hotel.

# 32

# Tokat

Tokat was my next stopping-place and its principal historical monuments are all Turkish – Seljuk and Ottoman – although its history is much older. It is 54 kilometres (34 miles) from Niksar, across the broad valley of the Kelkit, then up a 300-metre (1,000-foot) escarpment back into the hills. Across these hills the traveller then descends into a small, pretty gorge whose greenness is a contrast to much of the country through which I had travelled until then: the Yeşil Irmak or Green River lives up to its name. A dramatic ridge of rock crowned by the remains of an ancient citadel forms the backdrop to the city.

Tokat was a centre of the Danishmendids before the coming of the Seljuk Turks. Danishmend (a learned man) gave the name to his descendants, the Danishmendids, who controlled much of central Anatolia in the eleventh and twelfth centuries. They took Tokat from the Christians in the eleventh century when the Byzantine Empire was being steadily eroded on all sides before its final collapse. During the thirteenth century Tokat was to feature in the internecine struggles of the Seljuk princes.

The Seljuks who appeared on the scene in the eleventh century and collapsed before the Mongols in the thirteenth, left behind an imposing legacy of government and architecture. They ruled over a polyglot population of Christians (the Byzantines), Armenians, Greek, Syrians, and Iranians. At its greatest extent the Seljuk Empire stretched from Afghanistan to central Turkey, from the Caucasus to the Mediterranean, and the whole was divided into a number of sultanates or provinces. The Sultanate of Rum covered only that part of the empire in the Anatolian peninsula and came to be called Turkey during the period of Seljuk power.

In 1243 the Seljuks were defeated by the Mongols at the battle of Kose Dagh, which lies between Erzincan and Sivas. Before the Seljuk leader, Sultan Kaykhusraw, went to meet the Mongols in battle he placed his treasure and harem in the fortress of Tokat for safety, as it had been a key stronghold throughout Seljuk times. After his defeat the Sultan escaped back to Tokat where he collected his treasure and fled to Ankara. The Mongol period which followed was comparatively brief; then, during the fourteenth century, the Ottoman Turks became the predominant power throughout Anatolia.

Originally the citadel was fortified as the ancient Dazimon, guarding the approach to the sanctuary of the great Anatolian Earth Mother or Ma (appropriately to English ears) at Comana Pontica some 10 kilometres (6 miles) to the north. With the coming of the Byzantines and Christianity worship of the Earth Mother ceased, and the original town which grew up beneath the impressive rock citadel was Byzantine.

The remains of the ancient fortress, a 28-tower castle, were rebuilt by the Byzantines and Seljuks and, later, the Ottomans. Most of the surviving monuments in the city date from the Seljuk and early Ottoman period. A fine twelfth-century Seljuk bridge crosses the Yesil Irmak and there are mosques dating from the twelfth, sixteenth and seventeenth centuries.

It is strange how money values change. I had an excellent meal for which I was charged TL 2,000: I thought this expensive! In fact, by British standards, it was very cheap, but by then I had become so used to Turkish prices that I was almost tempted to protest. I was no longer translating Turkish lira into English pounds. There were in Tokat unmistakable signs of the tourist influence, or so it seemed. I found a pub whose layout and decor were more reminiscent of a German rather than Turkish place of entertainment. Later, I got into conversation with the man at the next table who turned out to be a friend or relative of the proprietor; he was on holiday from Germany where he had lived and worked for 15 years. The German factor again!

I stumbled upon a dye factory when I looked through an archway to discover a large dirty courtyard with an upper balcony running round its four sides. Great vats of dye occupied half the area while hanging from poles stretched across the top of the open courtyard were newly-dyed cloths out to dry. I was welcomed and given tea as though I had been expected; then a young man volunteered to show me round. It was an intriguing factory and I doubt the method of dyeing had altered in generations. In small rooms off the upper balcony I watched men with woodcuts dip these and make patterns on the cloth, superimposing one woodcut with a different coloured dye in the spaces left by the previous one. It is always a pleasure to watch a skill and the speed with which they built up a complicated pattern with a number of woodcuts each dipped in a different colour was breathtaking. In no time at all, at least to my unpractised eye, an entire cotton headscarf had been decorated in a dozen colours and hung up to dry.

While I was taking a picture of the museum, which is housed in a medieval *medresseh* (school), I was approached by a youth intrigued as always by the sight of my camera. He was a student at the university and wanted me to be a pen-friend from England. Bilal Gaglar was his name, one more addition to the list of new correspondents I had accumulated. Strangely, he didn't think to ask me to take his photograph.

Much of the old town of Tokat stretches up the side of the hill towards the grim rock citadel above. It consists of winding streets, alleyways and cobbled lanes; the upper storeys of the houses overhang the streets below so that these are often in deep shadow unless the sun is exactly overhead. The walls of houses were frequently decorated with red and green peppers strung out to dry for later use. I found a rare antique shop but there was nothing I wanted, although I was kept assiduously supplied with tea for half an hour while one item after another was brought out for my inspection. Amongst the maze of little streets I came upon a tiny, medieval mosque with an elegantly decorated dome inside. It was tucked away in a corner to serve a small segment of the population from the nearby twisting streets.

Later that day, back in the beer parlour, I had a long conversation with the German-speaking friend of the proprietor, principally about unemployment in Turkey. This was a frequent theme: the reason why so many Turks worked in Germany or sought work elsewhere in Europe, a point that was made more than once in connection with the electioneering already in progress for the November polls. Almost nightly, Prime Minister Özal was to be seen on television addressing the nation. Those Turks with whom I discussed the election showed a remarkable restraint about their politicians rather than any signs of overt enthusiasm.

The centre of the town has one of the most elegant tea-gardens I found anywhere in Turkey and I spent much time there. Part of it was a *restoran* and conkers from the overhanging trees were then falling, so that a sudden sharp crack on the ground and once on my head as I sat at table were reminders of approaching autumn. I got into conversation with a young Kurd. He came from Diyarbakir in eastern Turkey and was studying at the university. He was intensely nationalistic about his part of Turkey in comparison with Tokat where he was studying, but when I questioned him about the Kurdish problem in

Turkey he became cautious. We had a fast dictionary conversation which he lapped up, frequently snatching the dictionary from me to make a point. His enthusiasm reminded me of the school-teacher Gulci-han in Hacilar.

When he had gone to join some friends I watched with distaste a group of elderly women tourists, all American, who descended upon my tea-garden to make loud comments as they compared Tokat with the other places their bus had taken them to visit. I did not like them. Travel requires the traveller to imbibe the atmosphere of a place and I do not believe you can do this simply by coming to see things, especially as part of a group. It is necessary to sit and do nothing, as I frequently did. Invariably in such circumstances Turks approached me and we talked, so the doing, the understanding, was brought to me by my own inactivity.

I stayed three days in Tokat and on my last day, which turned out to be especially hot, I walked and climbed the ridge of rocks upon which the remains of the great fortress glower down upon the city below. Walking up through the old town I came first through an extensive cemetery spread out over the hillside. Then I ascended the ridge and worked my way back until I was right above the centre of the old town, before descending again down a steep gully under the castle to the top end of a little indeterminate street. A woman in purdah pointed the way for me.

That evening I had supper in the open *restoran* of the tea-garden and found myself shivering in a sudden drop in temperature. Then, quite late, as I went back to my hotel two young men approached me and asked in English if I would join them and their friends for tea back in the garden I had just left. They were teachers, they told me, attending a two-week conference in Tokat. They took me to a table at which five girls were sitting. They were all primary teachers at the same conference, two of whom spoke quite good English and a third French. All seven proceeded to question me as to my views about Turkey, democracy, the role of the military, Mrs Thatcher, the European Community, the USSR, President Reagan. One of the young men insisted he was a fascist, at which the others laughed, so I suggested that I was a Maoist.

Most Turks with whom I discussed politics were to the right of a fairly right-wing centre, or so it seemed. This at least was true of their ideas about foreign policy, perhaps not surprisingly considering Turkey's ancient enmity with Russia and the presence of large US NATO forces in the country. It was the first time that I had sat in a public place talking with a number of pretty Turkish girls who clearly belonged to the modern enfranchised Turkey and were prepared to talk freely. It was certainly a change. They demonstrated great curiosity about my trip and all of them wanted me to take away a good impression of Turkey.

# 33

# *'Veni, vidi, vici'*

When I came to leave Tokat I realised that I was approaching the end of my journey. Ahead of me were perhaps another half-dozen stops before I reached the coast at Carşamba. I took a *dolmus* from Tokat to Pazar, which was 22 kilometres (14 miles) away – I was feeling lazy – because I wanted to visit the Seljuk caravanserai, Hatun Hani, a massive thirteenth-century edifice though crumbling in decay. The little town was a busy, bustling place but without a hotel and I wandered round, an object of considerable curiosity. The Yeşil Irmak is still a small river here and lives up to its name: it is swift-running and the waters are green.

Such places present a strange mixture of old and new. Men were repairing telephone wires, and many tractors were in evidence, most having been driven into town by farmers on errands who used them as cars. There were several mechanical repair shops in the centre of the small town and, as far as I could judge, these were almost exclusively used for tractor maintenance. (A mechanical engineer with whom I spoke told me that Turkey was a maintenance and spare parts paradise for any company dealing with tractors since these were driven so fiercely and used so hard that the parts constantly wore out, broke or were otherwise destroyed before their time and required replacements.) Much of the town was crumbling, the houses in need of repairs, with wall plaster off in patches to reveal the wood pillars and slats behind, while many buildings urgently needed a fresh coat of paint. The generally run-down air suggested shortage of money for the most elementary repairs. Some of the roads were up, the town was dusty and messy. Yet a considerable amount of building was in progress alongside the dilapidation. It was as if, side by side, one part of the town was living in a past of poverty while immediately next door new wealth was responsible for fresh construction. The municipal council was busy with ditches for new drains. As always the tea-houses had a full complement of determined 'fixtures', all men; without exception women wore headscarves and many of them automatically took one side of the cloth in their teeth at sight of a stranger.

From Pazar I went to Turhal, also by *dolmus*. On this occasion the driver took on a very full load of passengers and I noticed a contrast in courtesies in the way men treated old and young women. They always made seats available to the old women, many of whom had large bundles to accommodate, but were often brusque with younger women, who had to squeeze into corners as best they could.

At first Turhal looked uninteresting. Yet in a single afternoon of wandering I was hailed and given more glasses of tea than in almost any other place I could remember. There were real contrasts between the givers and, as always, I was tempted to distinguish between those whose primary motive was courtesy to a stranger and those for whom it was curiosity to discover my origins and business. On one occasion two elderly men invited me with exquisite courtesy to join them outside a shop and I sat for half an hour chatting before they asked any probing questions at all. That, indeed, was a record. On another occasion, however, the experience was the reverse. This time my host had spent years in Germany and insisted upon questioning me with a determination which went beyond the bounds of curiosity into rudeness. In part it was his nature, but he also wanted to demonstrate to several cronies who had at once joined us that he spoke German and could make contacts in a way they could not. It was an occasion which brought home to me the inadequacy of my Turkish. I would have loved to be more fluent in the language, for then I would have used it to speak with the others and cut out the officious interpreting man who was my host. But despite nearly three months in the country my Turkish was still at the elementary phrase stage, a fact that made me ashamed. I had got stuck and could only comfort myself with the reflection, which was not necessarily true at all, that were I to stay in Turkey for another three months I would make a breakthrough to a new plane of understanding and speaking. Whether this would have been the case is another matter.

Turhal had also been a fortress of the Pontic kings, the ancient Gaziura, and had some ruins perched on its citadel though not much else to see that was old. The Yeşil Irmak runs between deep banks and must become a swollen torrent here during the rains or when the winter snows melt. I ate in what appeared to be the best *restoran* in town and both the food and service were awful, a most unusual experience. I awoke when it was still dark to the first calls to prayers and, though

I had given Kayseri top marks for the quality of the muezzin, calls this one artist in Turhal was in the first rank. When I came downstairs to leave the hotel the next morning I heard my name being spoken and discovered the receptionist and several men examining my passport and trying to pronounce the English. They looked momentarily sheepish to be caught out but relaxed as soon as I offered to give a lesson in English pronunciation.

Zile is visible from miles away over the plain, the long yellow walls and towers of its citadel-top fortress catching the sun as they dominate the red-roofed town below. I found a hotel beneath the steep hill of the citadel with a *hamam* (Turkish baths) behind it, and sat for a while talking with the receptionist while my room was prepared. This was on the top floor and gave me a superb view across the plain where Caesar fought his battle 2,000 years ago. Large plane trees in the street just reached the top windows and I could reach out to pluck a leaf.

It was market day in the town and as elsewhere I found streets entirely devoted to a single craft: one had nothing but small iron foundries, another was all clothes. I sat in a café to drink a Fanta which I did not want while I changed the film in my camera. A big fat man came puffing into the café, where he lowered his bulk into a chair before taking out a large silk handkerchief to mop his brow. He was an Italian and he was perspiring from the effort of climbing the citadel. He explained that he had come to see Caesar's column up on the citadel and I believe his sole purpose in visiting Zile was to establish to his own satisfaction the Italianate nature of Julius Caesar. Nothing else interested him. When he had recovered he departed and I watched him get into a large Mercedes which I had noticed earlier and drive out of the town.

Zile is an enchanting place in which to wander. The town is in the form of a circle with the citadel in the centre and though it is not particularly large I got lost more than once in its maze of streets. In a small bustling open fruit and vegetable market next to an old mosque I was invited to sit by a stall and given peaches to eat before I climbed the hill to the citadel. A young man with a guidebook in several languages sat near the entrance to the castle grounds, and he offered to come round with me, making sure that I saw the Roman column on which had been inscribed Caesar's laconic *'Veni, vidi, vici'*. It was in 47 BC that Caesar defeated King Pharnakes II, the son of Mithridates VI Eupator, when he attempted to regain the Pontic throne. The battle was fought on the plains beyond the town, which was then called Zela.

That battle, in which Caesar achieved a smashing victory in only four hours' fighting, finally brought the long Mithridatic wars to an end.

I found a tiny beer parlour (the name seems more appropriate than pub for such Turkish establishments, since clients always sit at tables) and had a beer before setting off to circle the town. Zile looked prosperous: there was a good deal of building in progress and I suspect it aims to make itself a more attractive stopping-place for the tourist trade. It certainly has an excellent setting, quite apart from its associations with Caesar.

It seemed odd to be in a town whose inhabitants were so ready to mention the dead Caesar; on five occasions when I got into conversations I was told of his battle and reference was made to his famous message of '*Veni, vidi, vici*'. The people of the town were clearly very proud of their most famous figure, or perhaps they were just getting into practice for a tourist trade to come.

That evening, after meandering in the depths of the town, where the upper storeys of the houses overhang the streets below, I found myself going round in circles, twice coming back to a corner whose increasing familiarity suggested that I had lost my sense of direction. So I followed a new road but after a while realised I was heading into the country. I retraced my steps past a young man and woman who were sitting outside their house. They greeted me and the man invited me into their high-walled garden to inspect his tomato crop, which was quite extensive. Two more women appeared: by their appearance I judged them to be his mother and her sister. They asked if I could take their photograph – I had been well and truly trapped – and when I produced my camera they smiled in a kind of gentle triumph: they had been correct in their guess. So I pointed to a wall where the sun shone and as we went round an angle of the house towards it a great guard dog on a long chain snarled and leapt towards me. The oldest of the women told it to shut up with an amused gesture and I lined them up for the picture. The women became very excited and wanted to make certain that I would send each of them a copy of the picture from England, which I promised to do.

I explained that I was lost and the young man said he would take me back to the citadel on his scooter. Almost at once as we rode through the narrow streets I glimpsed the citadel between houses and in no time at all we were in the small market square by the mosque. Adnan was the young man's name and he now accompanied me back up to the citadel and showed me proudly round it. We stood on the battlements looking over the plain of Zela and then he took me to the

Roman column. 'I will show you', he said, '*Veni vidi, vici*'. I peered long and carefully at the worn marble. I could distinguish the name, Caesar, and managed to find a *vici* but try as I might I could find neither a *Veni* nor a *vidi*. I had a faint suspicion, no doubt unjustified, that Caesar's column has been tampered with over the years.

I said goodbye to Adnan, who went off on his scooter, and found my way back to the beer parlour for a drink before my evening meal. Only when I was sitting over my beer did I realise that I had missed the opportunity to take a photograph of one of the dogs – chained – which had been so persistent a part of my travels. I never did get a picture of an Anatolian shepherd dog.

The stars still shone in the window when the early call to prayers went up. One old minaret was level with my hotel window and not more than 50 metres distant so that the call to prayers had the immediate effect of waking me. It was answered across the town and for five minutes the wailing, haunting noise announced the beginning of a new day. Below, a huge truck started up its engine and then the birds came to life. The big trees in the road outside the hotel were full of birds. First a number of small hooded crows circled in the high-light, cawing insistently to one another; these were then followed by the twittering of innumerable sparrows which had congregated in the tree beneath my window, and these in turn were succeeded by the wood-pigeons who cooed steadily for five minutes to stop as though on a signal when it became one degree lighter. And high up, circling in the now rapidly increasing light, were perhaps a dozen taper-winged hawks. The bright morning air had the early bite of autumn.

In the street below the town came to life. Just outside the hotel was a tea-garden and already it was busy. Shopkeepers put their wares out on the pavements and sprinkled water to keep down the dust. When I was ready to depart and had paid the hotel I had a glass of tea in the garden outside the hotel and almost at once was joined at my table by a loudmouthed, unkempt, half-mad individual who kept moving his face close to mine and then shouting. Such people are not easy to deal with but I watched him unmoved until other men from nearby tables came and told him to go away; then they apologised for his behaviour. I set off for Amasya.

# 34

# Amasya

The ancient city of Amasya has one of the most spectacular settings anywhere in Turkey. On the western side the great crags of the gorge rise sheer to a jagged ridge on which sit the remains of what was originally a Hellenistic castle and in the cliff-face are carved the rock caves of the Pontic kings. To the east the parallel hills, though less sheer, are grand enough to make the whole effect awe-inspiring. The city clusters tightly in the gorge on either side of the Yeşil Irmak. Along the river the wheels of the watermills creak, and beneath the rock caves on the west bank the old wooden houses lean over the water's edge. Originally the town lay beneath the tombs, guarded by walls which descended to the river from the great castle above. Later, in Seljuk times, Amasya spread to the eastern side of the Yeşil Irmak.

Although it no longer sits astride the great trade route from Samsun on the Black Sea to Sivas and Baghdad, Amasya is still a bustling city of importance, a market town and the capital of a rich agricultural province of the same name. Its monuments stretch back over a period of 2,500 years, though the majority which have survived are Seljuk, Mongol and Ottoman.

I had quite a search for a hotel for these were not situated on the main street. Then I found two in a small square facing the river: the first was full, but in the second I secured a room with a tiny balcony overlooking the tree-covered square below, where I could sit to watch the tea-house opposite. Amasya was the last city of any importance on my route and I was to stay there for three days. I found a *restoran* with a balcony above the river where I could watch the green waters of the Yeşil Irmak flowing swiftly towards me and boys leaping between the bases of the supports of the bridge upstream which the low waters had uncovered. Tucked away beyond the large town hall I discovered the expensive Amasya Turban Hotel (*Turistik*) where I took supper one night when a large party of *Is Bank* employees were having their

172

annual night out: a master of ceremonies organised them and, gradually, as they unwound he persuaded them on to the floor to dance. The music became increasingly lively although the dancing was most exciting when the men danced alone. Most of the women wore dresses of appalling style, a fashion rather like a sort of dumpy British 'new look' of the late 1940s. I rarely saw women either well or elegantly dressed except when they wore traditional clothes. At a small table near me a young English couple spent their entire meal each engrossed in a book, only looking up to eat or exchange a monosyllable. I hope they enjoyed their holiday together.

The adventurer, Mithridates I, made the fortress of Amaseia his capital and founded the Pontic kingdom which was to last for more than 200 years before the whole region finally fell under Roman control. Sometimes known a 'Cappadocia on the Sea', the kingdom of Pontus had been greatly extended by the second century BC under Mithridates V (the Great). Its last king, Mithridates VI Eupator, claimed descent from the first Mithridates and Darius. He was a legendary figure whose death was greeted by the Romans as though they had won a great victory. He succeeded to the Pontic throne at the age of 11 (in 120 BC) but his guardians wanted to assassinate him so he became a wanderer, a fugitive in his own kingdom, where he learnt disguise, deceit and hardship at an early age, changing his sleeping place every night for fear of those who would kill him. He grew to heroic stature and was renowned for his physical accomplishments whether as sportsman, fighter, gourmet or womaniser. He was ruthless and despotic so that even those closest to him lived in fear. He studied poisons to inure himself against their effects and to know which ones to use for those he would eliminate. He was a man of boundless energy and it was this rather than statesmanship which enabled him to expand his kingdom as he did. Sometimes he would wander incognito through the land, all of whose many languages he is said to have mastered. He was to give more trouble to the Romans as they expanded eastwards than any other opponent until the Parthian wars.

Most of the centres of population in Pontus were strongholds built round rock fortresses, citadels rather than towns. They were needed. Mithridates VI expanded Pontus throughout his reign, extending his power as far as the Greek kingdom of the Bosporus and to Lesser Armenia, and at the height of his power he ruled from the north to the south shores of the Black Sea and far into Armenia. He recruited from the mouth of the Danube to the Caucasus and the Caspian and for a time his fleet controlled the Black Sea.

During his first war against the Romans (88–84 BC) Mithridates VI massacred as many as 150,000 Italian settlers in his lands, and his ruthless despotism drove many of his supporters to join Rome in fear. As a result, he came to terms with Sulla and became a client of Rome but not for long. There were to be two more Mithridatic Wars and in the final one he was opposed by Pompeius (the Great). In his final battle against the Romans at Nicopolis on the banks of the Yeşil Irmak he was routed and had to flee with only two attendants and a concubine who had fought at his side dressed in male attire, and he ended his long reign of 57 years as he had begun it, wandering, in search of supporters. He tried to raise another army but he was surrounded by treachery and was deserted. Finally, when his own son, who had revolted, demanded his death, he committed suicide but only after he had forced his retinues of concubines to precede him in drinking poison. He died in 63 BC, 26 years after first taking the field against the Romans, a fierce, treacherous grey-haired old man of 67. He has sometimes been seen as an early nationalist opposing the imperialism of Rome, although the thought is unlikely to have occurred to him.

Strabo, the geographer, was born in Amasya in 64 BC and describes the gorge with its citadel and rock tombs much as it appears today except that the castle walls are now only ruins. Before the city became the capital of Pontus it was taken by Alexander the Great. It was made into a Byzantine bishopric and became part of the late Byzantine kingdom of Trebzond until it was captured by the Danishmendid Turks in 1075, subsequently passing to the Seljuks, the Mongols and finally the Ottomans. Like so many other cities in Turkey the history can be uncovered layer by layer back to antiquity.

I found a barber's shop near my hotel and had a haircut, by then much needed, and also had my beard shaved off. This operation was watched with amusement and interest by several customers, who said they wanted to see what I looked like underneath. With the courtesy which always matched their curiosity my onlookers insisted that the removal of the beard had also removed ten years from my age. I do not really like a beard and felt fresh and clean without it. I had grown it as a convenience rather than for any other reason but now that it had gone I also felt that I was coming to the end of my journey. Back at my hotel the old man in reception did not at first recognise me.

I climbed through steep streets at the north-west end of the town and among the trees came upon a dilapidated park, its stonework neglected and falling to pieces, weeds growing up through what had once been elegant paving, and only the inevitable statue of Attatürk looking as though it had been cared for in the preceding 20 years. There was an old man there gathering herbs from the ground under the trees. He came to talk and lamented the neglect of the little park which, he said, could be beautiful. I agreed and we smoked a contemplative cigarette together before he went off on his business and I descended again through the twisting streets. I inspected a pretty little mosque and then when several small children began following me, chanting, '*What is your name?*', was surprised by an old woman who called fiercely to them to behave and leave me in peace. I saluted her and went down to find a *Fici Bira* sign.

After visiting the rock tombs I climbed the steep gully to the high ridge which dominates the gorge where the extensive remains of the citadel walls follow the contours of the hillside facing west. I became stuck on a last, sheer bit of rock but a Turkish youth appeared on a nearby abutment and, spurred by an audience, I managed to finish the climb in style. He came to talk and then guided me all over the remnants of the castle: the tunnel which leads back down to the river for water, the cannon – now ornamental and fixed in cement – which overlooks the Yeşil Irmak and the gorge below. Then I took a long walk back behind the ridge to come round to the town a more gentle way.

In the evening light just before sunset I climbed again to the highest of the great rock tombs and sat on the edge of the rock viewing the length of Amasya stretching along the banks of the river below. It was a lovely sight with the glinting waters of the Yesil Irmak separating the two halves of the town, the red roofs of the old houses soft in the evening light. A small band marched through the town, its drums and trumpets echoing up the gorge. Perhaps it was a segment of the Turkish Salvation Army, I thought. It was the only time on the whole journey that I missed a companion who would have appreciated the irony of the thought.

# 35

# Down to Çarşamba

At the north end of Amasya on the road out of town is the Mosque of the Twisted Minaret, dating from 1247. Its interior is plain, almost severe, and in a corner there are the remains of a staircase leading to what was a private pew belonging to some past Seljuk grandee. In a nearby rock face is a small, less magnificent tomb than those which can be seen high up the great cliff on the other side of the gorge. From this point I set out on the road to Tasova.

Between Amasya and Tasova the Yeşil Irmak drops about 120 metres (400 feet). The road is always in sight of the river, which rushes and bubbles its course over rocks, twists and turns, sometimes dropping out of sight behind high banks as the road climbs, sometimes looking gentle and almost sluggish and, more often than not, a shining emerald green. Tasova is a pretty little town with a wide open main street and a backdrop of sharp hills, their starkness softened by occasional trees, either lone sentinels or clusters of dark green – sheep country again.

After a search which involved a pleasant interlude drinking tea with a willing helper we found the manager of the hotel, which was locked, and I booked in. Near the hotel, side by side, were a tea-house and then a *lokanta* and I sat outside for a drink before seeking food. A band, or more correctly, a man beating a drum and a boy playing a flute, kept up non-stop monotonous music, although this possessed a compelling, rhythmic attraction of its own. They sat at a little table just outside the *lokanta* and when I had finished my tea I went to take their photograph. They enjoyed that, although the head of the man with the drum remained obstinately bathed in deep shade from the roof of the building above despite my signals for him to lean forward. Then he waved me to a seat and ordered tea. They stopped playing for a while to talk with me but soon they started up again – the music sounded much the same – and men entering the *lokanta* dropped notes for small amounts of money, usually TL 100, on the table beside them.

I, too, went into the *lokanta* and sat at the only empty table I could find: at once a man came to shake my hand and sit with me to talk. He was unusually smart, in collar and tie and well-creased suit. He asked me what I would like to eat and called instructions to the waiters. Food was brought at once, better fare than usual, and then I noticed that men leaving only shook hands with the proprietor at the door: no one appeared to pay anything for his meal. I had walked in on a private affair, the entertainment for a wedding that must have taken place elsewhere. Embarrassed, I began to excuse myself to the man at my table, but he laughed and called over another man and together they welcomed me, and insisted how delighted they were that I could join them to celebrate. So I enjoyed my meal and told them of my travels in Turkey. When I left the man at the desk where normally I would have paid offered me a bowl of sweets and shook my hand: I was just one of the many guests who were coming and going all the time. Outside the two-man band had never ceased playing and they, too, had been hired for the occasion.

As with the Kizil Irmak at the beginning of my journey so with the Yeşil Irmak at the end a dam had been constructed to create a great lake which had altered the nature of the river valley. A long walk through the hills, assisted by tractor lifts, and fierce Anatolian shepherd dogs barking their warnings at me, though luckily always from a distance, gave me one last feel of the bleak open land that is the backbone of Turkey.

The dam barrage below Ayvaçik with a height of between 25 and 30 metres (80 and 100 feet) lies some 12 kilometres (8 miles) south of Carşamba and has created a long lake like a Scottish loch which winds its way back into the purple hills. Like the far larger lake which stretched back for perhaps 50 kilometres (30 miles) from Kolay near the mouth of the Kizil Irmak so must this smaller lake have disrupted an entire way of life.

Since Amasya I had been conscious of an unmistakable autumnal chill in the air, for the weather was about to break, although the middle of the day could still be very hot. The lake was unbelievably blue. It sparkled under the early autumn sun and small fish leaped upon its surface.

There was a busy market in Ayvaçik, which clusters on a shelf beside the newly-created lake. Tractors and minibuses had come in from many destinations bringing people to the market, which was set out under huge canvas umbrellas or awnings stretched between buildings down steep little dirt streets that ran from the road where all the vehicles had parked down to the water's edge. It was a colourful, tight-packed market of garish plastic utensils, children's toys, endless lines of women's and children's clothes dazzling with their many hues and, as always, farm implements and tools. I wandered round, hardly noticed for once in the bustling, bargaining crowds and then found a tiny *lokanta* near the water's edge where I ate mutton stew. Two large open boats powered by motors were filling with passengers to cross the lake to settlements on the other side, while a solitary cow, tethered by the waterside, chewed or bellowed alternately but was ignored. I found a tea-garden which overlooked the section of the market devoted to clothes, line upon line of them flapping lazily just beneath me, stirred, though not much, by a faint breeze from the lake. Three men came to share my table for all the other tables were fully occupied, but apart from a curt greeting from one of them they ignored me, engrossed in some private discussion of their own. Their abruptness was in startling contrast to the more usual determination to get into conversation. They left before I did without a goodbye, which was also unusual, yet when I went to pay for my several drinks I discovered that they had done so for me. Even unfriendly Turks maintained their reputation for hospitality to a stranger.

Çarşamba is dusty, messy and ramshackle yet it shops were crowded with goods and the town was vibrant with activity. It is divided by the Yeşil Irmak, wide and no longer green, with mud banks breaking the shallow waters. I found a small hotel overlooking the river and the next morning watched men take horse-drawn carts on to the mud banks and shovel full loads of it into their vehicles, though what they wanted it for I did not discover. I stayed in Çarşamba for two days, since I had a last trip to make.

That evening I wandered upstream and just out of the town came to an open area of flat grass alongside the river-bank which provided room for football fields. Great clouds were building up above the hills ready for rain. I watched a youth of perhaps 17 casting a fishing net in the shallow muddy water. He wore only shorts and had a body like a pocket Hercules; a small boy of about 11 attended upon him and when they came up the bank they stopped to greet me and talk, or rather the small boy did the talking while the older youth stood by grinning amiably. I took their photograph, the smaller boy holding up a fish no larger than a sardine, the prize of their catch. Then they walked back into the town, turning frequently to wave to where I sat smoking at the river's edge.

I had supper in an above-average *restoran* that overlooked a wide open space, hardly a square, which stretched down the hill to the bridge across the river. It pelted with rain throughout the meal, the first rain since I had been in Turkey, and rivulets of water careered down the steep road below the window where I ate, all the stonework of the buildings and roads glistening wet under the street lighting. Twice during a long meal a whirring noise announced the breakdown of generators and the town was plunged into darkness. Lamps and candles were produced and I had a rare fish meal composed of some of the best trout I have ever tasted: Turkish trout. Now all that remained for me to do was to close the circle.

# 36

# Closing the Circle

Like Bafra, Çarşamba lies about 20 kilometres (12 miles) inland from the Black Sea, for over the centuries the waters of the Yeşil Irmak have brought down silt to build up a V-shaped headland where the river meets the sea. I proposed to complete my journey as I had begun it by walking along the Yeşil Irmak from Çarşamba to its mouth on the Black Sea shore. The weather had indeed changed and it was a chilly, overcast day with low clouds constantly threatening rain. Two bowls of hot soup were a more than usually appropriate breakfast and then, with fruit in my camera bag, I set off on my last walk. As I passed a tea-house, what had looked like a carelessly discarded brown rug lying in the gutter leapt up to bite me and luckily got the bag slung from my shoulder instead. It was a young Alsatian, a mere toy creature compared with the Anatolian shepherd dogs I had now left behind in the hills. I managed to lose my way, taking what appeared to be the correct dirt road along the river and for a time looking down a steep 15-metre (50-foot) bank to the swirling waters which had risen during the night following the heavy rains, but I soon came to a dead end and had to walk at right angles away from the river before I found the road to Kadilik, the last village on the way to the sea.

Like the Bafra headland, Çarşamba's was also an area of rich agricultural land. I walked steadily for three hours and then came to a roadside shop where I stopped for a cold drink just as it began to rain in earnest. After a while I decided to continue anyway and was soon soaked. A tractor and trailer came along and gave me a lift but the rain became so heavy that the driver stopped and the three of us – he had a teenage boy with him – sheltered under the trailer to smoke a cigarette while we waited for a break in the weather. When it had eased off we drove into Kadilik in a steady cold drizzle.

In the tea-house I was questioned as usual: what on earth was I doing getting soaked walking in such weather? There was nothing to do or see in Kadilik. So I fell into my wandering minstrel role and explained about the circle of my two rivers. I should only have completed my journey when I had reached the mouth of the Yeşil Irmak on the Black Sea and seen its lighthouse. This curious wish caused considerable amusement as I had guessed it would, and then a grinning farmer said he would take me there in his tractor and trailer. Remzi Kales was his name. He invited a friend along and the three of us set out, the friend and I standing in the empty trailer, Remzi at the wheel of his powerful tractor forcing it at speed along the dirt tracks which led to the sea. This was about 8 or 9 kilometres (5 or 6 miles) distant from the village. Eventually we left the paths and drove across soft sandy country of sparse, coarse grass, where scattered cows and horses were grazing. It was wild, flat land where tall reeds bent before the wind. We came to the small, undistinguished grey-white lighthouse, a replica of that on Bafra point and the tractor got stuck in thick soft sand. I got down to take a picture of Kales at the wheel and then both men posed on the steps of the lighthouse for another picture, though the light was so dull and poor that I doubted the end-product would be much good.

When we had freed the tractor we walked to the seashore by the mouth of the Yeşil Irmak and the friend, a small gnome-like man with laughing features, took my walking-stick, which he swung with panache. Why such a stick? So I told the story of the dogs and they questioned me about my trip and were intrigued to learn that I had started at Bafra, only 80 kilometres (50 miles) along the coast to the west. The sea was breaking in white frothing waves along the shore, and the line of the water beyond the breakers really did look black in contrast to the lighter, oily grey surface of the river, while overhead the clouds lowered more threatening than ever. My two friends were voracious for pictures so I photographed them individually and together; I set the camera for each in turn to take me posing with the other man, and finally I took them in a rice field as we walked back along the river towards the tractor.

We dropped off the friend at his house and then Remzi deposited me at the tea-house. He had made the trip solely for my benefit and his own amusement, and the two hours we had spent churning away over the thick sand or walking on the Black Sea shore had been amongst the most pleasant I could recall, a fitting end to a journey in which my encounters with Turks had been almost universally friendly. At the tea-house an officious friend came to tell me I should pay for the diesel fuel, but Remzi refused point-blank. I promised to send him the pictures on my return, we shook hands, and he roared off on his tractor. I waited for a while at the roadside until a *dolmus* with a great fat jolly driver arrived and I took this back to Çarşamba, my river circle completed.